DOLLY MADISON

DOLLY

MADISON

---

by JANE MAYER

Illustrated by WALTER BUEHR

Landmark BOOKS

RANDOM HOUSE · NEW YORK

CONTENTS

1. FAREWELL TO THE FAMILIAR

WHEN Dolly Payne was fifteen years old, she was told by her parents that nearly everything in her life was about to be changed. They were going to sell their Virginia plantation, they said, free their slaves and, with Dolly and her brothers and sisters, move north to far-away Philadelphia. They had always been land-owning, farming people. Now they were going to become city people. They were going to seek a new living in a new place. While doing it, they would adhere as firmly as ever to their Quaker principles and would also be able to give their children a sound religious education in the City of Brotherly Love.

In the year 1783, a young girl did not question her father's decisions. This was particularly true of a father like John Payne. He was

a serious man who had become a Quaker because his wife was a Quaker, a man who had
been Clerk of the Quakers' Cedar Creek Meeting, then Elder, then Minister. He lived his
beliefs as firmly as he held them. A young girl
did not question her mother's decisions, either,
when mother and father stood in complete
accord.

But Dolly did not want to question or object to this determination to move. She herself
felt strongly about it, and her feelings were
strong in two exactly opposite ways.

She certainly had no desire to leave the
state of Virginia. For although she had been
born in North Carolina in 1768, she had
moved when she was nine months old. And
all the rest of her life had been lived in Virginia. She knew and loved the Payne plantation called Scotchtown, with its broad
meadows, cultivated fields and blossoming
dogwood trees. She knew and loved most of
the family slaves, and the visitors from far off
who were so hospitably housed, and the
neighbors who came to call. She knew and
loved and would always remember the plantation house itself, that huge straight-lined
building of brick and clapboard, with its
many high-ceilinged rooms, its black marble

mantels imported from Scotland, its mysterious and fearful ancient dungeon.

Dolly also knew and cherished the wooded pathway to her Quaker school, the log schoolhouse, the hard schoolhouse benches and the drone of lessons. She liked her friends and their talk and games.

At home, she was familiar with and happy in plantation work, spinning, carding, weaving, soap-making, handling the keys of a storeroom to distribute supplies, handling them again when it was time for new supplies to be stored away.

But along with not wanting to give up the life she had lived, there was her curiosity and anticipation about the new life. She wanted to live in a city, to see what Philadelphia, described to her by her mother and brother, was like. She was eager to watch a mail coach arrive, to walk on cobbled streets, to hear nightwatchmen's cries or street vendors' cries, to shop at a big market, to observe busy, important men and well-dressed fashionable women. She longed to be part of a city where there were balls and theaters, cockfights, wrestling matches and horse races, even though she might not be allowed to go to any of these.

Dolly distributed supplies in the storeroom

As the tedious, difficult packing for the journey began, Dolly did not toss and turn at night and say, "How can I bear to leave all this at Scotchtown?" She did not cry and wail and object even in secret. She hated to leave, and yet she wanted to leave. She threw her energy into the preparations for departure.

Throughout her life there were to be many changes, many uprootings, and each was to be met the same way. Dolly clung to the old, while at the same time welcoming all that was new, adventurous and strange. For she would always hesitate, looking with affection at the known and familiar. But after the hesitation she would always go on, would like the new she found and would always return at some time to pick up the threads of the old.

She did not have to ask her parents why they were making the move. That problem had been discussed for years, at home, at the Cedar Creek Meeting of the Quakers, in groups of close acquaintances, and at Coles' Hills where her mother's parents lived. It was, quite simply, a question of slave-owning. Virginia law had for many years forbidden an owner to free his slaves. At that time Virginians thought plantations could not possibly operate without slaves—slaves to work the fields, harvest the crops, care for the horses, do the horseshoeing, the brick making, the carpentry, the meat curing and the hundreds of other necessary tasks. For each Virginia plantation was a unit in itself—farm, factory and home in one. A traveling cobbler might settle down there for a few days each year to

5

mend all the shoes. But, for the most part, little outside help could be counted on.

Against this need for slaves was the Quaker conviction that owning slaves was a great wrong. The convinced Quakers fought out this battle within their own minds until Virginia law finally permitted an owner to free his slaves if he wished to do so. Then it was up to each owner to act on this question as he pleased.

One of the first of the Virginia Quakers to be sure what he wanted to do was Dolly's father, John Payne. He was a man of stubborn, direct thought. If he believed something was right, he did it. If he believed it was wrong, he did not do it. He reasoned this way: He did not believe in slavery. Therefore he could not own slaves. Therefore he could not run a plantation. And if he could not run a plantation, he must find another way to earn a living for his wife and his children, Walter, William Temple, Dolly, Isaac, Lucy, Anna, Mary and John. He must sell his land and buildings, and use the money from the sale to set himself up in business. To go into business, he must be in a city. Philadelphia was big and thriving. The Paynes knew many peo-

6

ple there who would help him get started. John Payne had it all thought out.

It did not bother Dolly that her father had had no experience in business or that he knew nothing about city life and city expenses and

city ways. She had never had to worry about anything of this kind. She and her brothers and sisters had always had more than enough space, more than enough good food and more than enough of their simple, homespun clothing. They had had love and consideration from their parents. They had been able to lean on their parents and get help from them when they wanted it. Furthermore, in 1783, a Virginia girl of fifteen was a young woman.

7

Some even married at that age. All were expected to know the arts of housekeeping and to take on many of the responsibilities of these arts. Dolly had had good training and much practice. She was not afraid of work.

As the time to move approached, there seemed to be nothing to worry about in the future, except how to make friends in a new place, how to do her share of the work of moving, settling, and caring for the younger children, and how to have as much fun as possible.

Dolly, at fifteen, was fairly tall and she was slender. She walked with assurance. She had black curly hair, bright blue eyes and a nice warm smile. She had the very white skin that goes with her kind of coloring, but it had been kept whiter than would ordinarily have happened to the usual girl living on the usual plantation with the usual mother. Mrs. Payne had seen to that by making white mitts for her daughter's hands and a white linen mask to cover her daughter's nose and cheeks and chin. The mother had known that Dolly would wear the deep, protective Quaker bonnet and the ample gray Quaker dress. She had known that mask and clothes and gloves together would safeguard the girl's skin from the hot

8

Virginia sun. For once Mrs. Payne forgot that it was worldly and not like a Quaker to care so much for outward personal beauty. She had insisted that Dolly begin this protection as a little child and that she carry it through to young womanhood.

But there was one way in which Dolly herself had been worldly that her mother had not encouraged and had not shared. Perhaps her mother had not even known about it. Dolly's grandmother, her father's mother, was the one who had known and encouraged this. The grandmother gave the little girl a piece of jewelry which the old lady had owned for a long time. Since this grandmother was not a Quaker, she saw no harm in owning and wearing jewelry and felt that the child should have some. But the child already knew the Quaker principles of strict simplicity. She had two feelings about the "bauble" as she called it, just as she was later to have two feelings about moving away from Virginia. She knew she could not and should not wear it where it would show. Yet she could not bear to do without it. So she sewed it into a little bag and wore it on a string around her neck, hidden beneath her dress. She wore it this way for several years, happy that she had the

9

treasure, happy that she did not show it off. And then one day she lost it. She did not know where or when the string broke and the little bag fell off. She searched and searched and never found it. She talked about this bauble when she herself became as old as her grandmother had been. She still thought of it affectionately. It was another one of the threads of her early life that she never quite gave up. Possibly it was one of the reasons why jewelry was so important and pleasing to her when she was the wife of the President of the United States.

At fifteen, however, she was between the child who had lost the bauble and the woman who was to be First Lady. She had something of both these other two in her. In childishness she worried about how she would get along without Mother Amy, the slave who had been her nurse. In womanliness she worried about how her younger brothers and sisters would get along without Mother Amy who was still their nurse. Day after day Dolly watched while the papers were drawn up to give the slaves their freedom. Then came the time for Mother Amy's papers. The slave woman had a surprise for all of them. She said she would take her freedom, but that she would not leave them. She would accept a salary from Mr. Payne, but she would work for the family and care for them all just as she had done before.

Dolly looked at Mother Amy with love and with relief. It was still exciting to think of moving to Philadelphia. But it was a great comfort to know that this second mother would stay with the family to help them take what came, among new people and in new surroundings. Dolly was sure that she herself could take whatever came and that she would enjoy it.

2. A NEW WORLD

THE Revolutionary War had meant very little to Dolly Payne. This was partly because she was young while it was going on and partly because she lived on a plantation instead of in a city. But it was mostly because of her parents and their Quaker belief that war was wrong. During wartime a Quaker like John Payne could continue to grow his crops, attend and preach at meeting and care for those who were in need, but he could not fight. He could feel and argue for or against the British, but he could not take up arms without being "read out of meeting." And, to John Payne, his Quakerism was more important than anything else. So, while they were in Virginia and she knew nothing else, Quakerism was more important for Dolly, too.

But in Philadelphia, things were different. When the Payne family reached Philadelphia

after that long tiring coach journey, the war
was over and the treaty signed. But the marks
of the war were everywhere. The marks were
in the weary faces of people, in the bodies of
the wounded or crippled veterans, and in the
half-empty pockets of many of the citizens.
The marks were strongest in the talk that was
going around and in the questions that were
being asked. Were the states going to stick together now that the war was won? Could the
Continental Congress really do anything important, even anything as vital as raising
enough money for government needs?
Wouldn't the people be better off if they
appointed a king? Or could they be self-
governing?

At first, these questions drifted only vaguely
around young Dolly. She could not help being
aware of them, but, on the other hand, there
was much to do and see in Philadelphia and
there were many new people to make friends
with.

The task of setting up housekeeping in the
new way was a chore in itself. Instead of the
big plantation house, there was the usual
Philadelphia city house—narrow, two-and-a-
half stories high. Instead of the acres of land,
there was a small plot of ground. Instead of

the many huge high-ceilinged rooms, there were a few tiny low-ceilinged ones. There were no slaves, now, and only Mother Amy to help with the work. There were no storerooms bulging with home-cured hams. A great many other things that Dolly was used to were lacking.

But one could tumble out of the front door onto a brick-paved sidewalk and be in the middle of activity. One could walk back in the

In 1783 the Paynes moved to Philadelphia

14

house again and be in Mr. Payne's "shop." (He had, soon after their arrival, taken the money from the sale of the plantation and had set himself up in the starch business. Like most Philadelphians of the day, he had his office and business in the front ground-floor room of his home.) Or one could walk in either direction down the street and see other shops where there were elegant hats and dresses. Or, eager and curious, one could just stand on the sidewalk and watch carriages go by, bearing women who wore such creations. One could walk farther away to the market and examine foods not grown in Virginia, or walk to the river where the ocean-going vessels came to port and wonder what foods or dresses or letters or newspapers these ships had brought from Europe.

Dolly did all of these things and many more besides. She met girls her own age and boys her own age and older. She went to picnics and teas and evening gatherings, and rode out to the country homes of her new friends. She entertained guests of her own at home. She went regularly to Quaker Meeting, walking to and from meeting with these friends and others. She began to feel as if she had always lived in Philadelphia. She grew taller and prettier—so pretty that the young men would turn to watch her as she walked by in her long gray Quaker clothes and her demure sugar-scoop Quaker bonnet.

Gradually, though, as she became accustomed to the gaiety and the sights, the crowds and the companions, she began to hear more of what the people of Philadelphia were actually saying about those years after the war and about their fears and hopes for the new nation. Along with everyone else, she knew that the Constitutional Convention was going to meet in Philadelphia, that George Washington had said that the thirteen states were "united only by a rope of sand," and that something must be done to create a strong national government.

Dolly was nineteen years old and had lived in Philadelphia for four years when the Constitutional Convention assembled there in May, 1787. Along with the other Philadelphians, she could share the excitement of watching the delegates arrive—Washington, escorted ceremoniously and cheered on by the shouting of citizens and the ringing of bells; Alexander Hamilton, coming from New York; Edmund Randolph, the Governor of Virginia. She could observe with new eyes their fellow-townsmen who were delegates—Benjamin Franklin and Robert Morris. She could share equally with everyone the interest in seeing James Madison, a short good-looking young man from Virginia who was known to be a bookish and brilliant political thinker.

After the Convention had begun, Dolly could be sorry, along with many others, that all the Convention proceedings were so secret and that no one could find out from day to day what took place. But Dolly would learn, many years later, that this same James Madison had been the one delegate to keep a full daily record of everything that was suggested, vetoed or approved at the Convention. In less years than that, she would learn how he had sponsored the "Virginia Plan," the pattern for the Constitution, and why he was called "Father of the Constitution." She would learn, too, why he was respected for his great knowledge of affairs of the United States and why he was loved for his modesty about his knowledge.

The Constitutional Convention proceeded slowly, lasting from May until September. When the Constitution was finished, the next step was to have it ratified by at least nine states, so that it could become law. The battle lines for and against it drew up. The battle to ratify the Constitution was for a strong central government as opposed to a loose League of States; for a republic or representative type of government, as against a weak organization with each man for himself. For a while, it looked as if real union was impossible.

Then the New York newspapers began to publish a series of articles by Alexander Hamilton, James Madison and John Jay. These articles—powerful, clear and simple—explained why Confederacy, or a League of States, had not worked and would not work, why there was a need for federal authority and why the new Constitution fitted the best principles of republican government.

The people of Philadelphia and elsewhere read and discussed these articles. They read and discussed them again when the essays came out in book form as *The Federalist.* Throughout the thirteen states arguments for and against the Constitution were hot. No one could be entirely unaware of what was going on.

At this time Thomas Jefferson wrote to James Madison: "Educate and inform the whole mass of the people. Enable them to see that it is to their interest to preserve peace

and order, and they will preserve them."
Jefferson was right in this as in so many other
things. The people read and listened, and the
Constitution was ratified.

The celebration in Philadelphia was magnificent. On July 4, 1788, throngs of people
crowded the narrow sidewalks and lined the
cobblestone streets to watch a procession of

Throngs watched the procession of floats go by

19

floats go by. For the moment, everyone was
in tune. They booed the float that had a
floundering, weak old ship, *Confederacy*.
They cheered the float that represented the
strong new ship, *Constitution*. No one who
knew Dolly Payne and her love of people and
excitement could doubt that she was in the
crowd.

Perhaps one good reason for any of the
Paynes to go out into crowds those days was
that things were not going well at home.
There was still warmth and affection among
the family members, still the usual bustle of
family affairs, but money problems had become very severe.

Life in Philadelphia had surprised them all
by being so much more expensive than life
on their plantation, Scotchtown. They had
been surprised, too, to find that a man who
had been a successful farmer did not know
how to be a successful businessman when he
was selling starch. John Payne was as industrious as he had been in Virginia, but instead
of making money, he lost it. The large family
moved from one small house to another and
to another again. But even so, the starch business in the first floor front room did not pros-

per. Debts began to pile up. John Payne was very quiet about his troubles. Yet his family knew how great the struggle was. Dolly tried to help him, but there was little that she could do.

3. MRS. TODD

DOLLY was not one to sit at home and brood. Rather, she was a person of action. And if she found herself in a situation where she could not act, she turned her attention to something else. Since she could not help her father in his money troubles, she went quietly on with her household chores. She also continued her gay social life as it had been before. She was twenty-one now and very popular. Several young men wanted to marry her. Many of her young women friends were already married. But Dolly was in no hurry to settle down. She said "no" to all her suitors. She said "no" quite often to the most persistent of them, John Todd, and John Todd went right on asking her. She continued to be merry and friendly and busy. Her blue eyes sparkled, and her black curls bobbed beneath the Quaker cap.

Then one day the business troubles got too big to be handled and the debts too big to be paid. Mr. Payne went into bankruptcy. This was a great enough blow for him and his family, but what followed was even worse for them. In the eyes of his fellow Quakers, his failure was a disgrace and the Quakers "read him out of meeting," forcing him to give up his membership in the church organization because he owed money that he could not pay.

Mr. Payne was not like Dolly. He *did* brood. Silent and hurt, he returned to his home. He went to his own room. He stayed in this room, week after week and month after month. The church to which he had given so much of his loyalty, energy and thought had turned him out. Because of this he seemed to have no wish to mingle with people or to lead any kind of a life.

Dolly's mother did not give in. Perhaps she did not know as well as Dolly how to be happy in almost all circumstances. But she did know how to make the best of things. She put her shoulder against misfortune and pushed with all her might. She would not allow her children to sink into the despair that had swallowed up their father. She knew that many other gentlewomen, because of crowded conditions in Philadelphia, were taking boarders into their homes. She decided that by doing the same she could earn a living and keep her family together. So, in some ways, the Payne family went on much as it had been before.

All this time John Todd continued to call on Dolly. When she finally said "yes," no one was terribly surprised. Todd was a good man. He was bright and honest and industrious. He was a religious Quaker of a fine Philadelphia family, and he was a lawyer who would no doubt make a success at law. He was also a gentle, loving and considerate person.

They were married in January, 1790, and two years later their first child, a son, was born. A little over a year after that, they had a second son. Their life was serene and quiet. But for a woman who could find so much pleasure in so many things it was exciting and joyous as well. Dolly marketed and sewed for her own family now. When she cooked and cleaned, it was in her own home. The furniture she polished was as fine as any in Philadelphia, and it was her own. The first floor room in her house was used as a law office by her own husband, a man who loved her and could take care of her. The two babies, who smiled when she smiled, were now not bothersome younger brothers and sisters, but were boys of her own. Dolly was content. Both her face and her figure grew fuller.

There were griefs in these pleasant years, too, but they were softened by circumstance. The death of Mr. Payne, Dolly's father, was not the great shock it might have been, for he had long since made himself into a shadowy figure by withdrawing so much from everyone's life. The death of Mother Amy was made easier to bear by the wonderfully loving thought she showed toward the Payne family. She had accepted her wages all through the Philadelphia days, but she had spent none of them. She willed the entire amount to Dolly's mother at a time when the Paynes were desperately in need of money.

In those same years, important things were happening throughout the world. People read about the events in the small newspapers. They received or wrote informative letters about them. And they noticed the events a little or a lot according to what kind of people they were and what their interests were.

To Dolly it was important when old Benjamin Franklin died and when the capital of the United States was moved from New York back to Philadelphia. It was important that

James Madison, serving in the House of Representatives, had much to do with adding the Bill of Rights to the Constitution. It was terribly important when her fifteen-year-old sister, Lucy, was married to a seventeen-year-old favorite nephew of President Washington. It

Jean Pierre Blanchard went up in a balloon

26

was important when a Frenchman named Jean
Pierre Blanchard went up in a balloon and
everyone, including Washington, turned out to
watch this amazing, impossible feat. Dolly had
a lot to talk about and hear about when the
French Republic was proclaimed and Louis
XVI executed, and when Washington was inaugurated for a second time.

And then in August, 1793, something happened that was immensely important for
everybody and horrible for everybody. An epidemic of yellow fever swept over Philadelphia.
It was the worst epidemic ever to strike any
American city. All life in the city stopped except to care for the sick, to run away in terror
from the sick, or to *be* one of the sick. Nothing was known of how the plague started, and
almost nothing was known of how to stop it.
Great numbers of people died and even
greater numbers fled from the town, carrying
strangely useless possessions with them, and not
knowing where they were going or who would
take them in. The panic was terrific.

The city became almost deserted. Jefferson,
writing again to James Madison, who had left
before the plague started, said: "I would really
go away, because I think there is rational
danger, but that I announced I should not go

An epidemic of yellow fever swept over Philadelphia

till the beginning of October, and I do not like to exhibit the appearance of panic. Besides that, I think there might be serious ills proceed from there being not a single member of the administration in place."

When it was seen that "bark" and "bleeding" would not cure the sick or that firing a cannon to clear the air of swamp vapors did not end the epidemic, John Todd insisted that Dolly leave Philadelphia with her two-year-old son, her infant son and her mother. Todd escorted the party to an inn not far away, a place called Gray's Ferry. Here in the country he felt they would be safer. But he would not stay with them. While others were running away from the plague, he returned to it, to do what nursing he could and what law work was necessary. Every once in a while he would visit his family at Gray's Ferry, and each time Dolly would beg him to stay there with them. Each time he refused because he felt he was so needed in town.

At length Todd's own parents became ill in Philadelphia. He stayed with them, nursed them, and when they died, buried them. By this time, his days and nights of work and worry had worn him out, and he, too, caught the fever.

He did not give in at once. He struggled back to Gray's Ferry and almost collapsed on the doorstep. When he saw Dolly's mother at the door he said, "I feel the fever in my veins. But I must see *her* once more."

Dolly heard his voice, ran down the stairs and caught him in her arms. He sagged to the floor, and they knew how ill he was. They also knew how swift and terrible this disease could be. They put him to bed and tried to nurse him. But a few hours later, John Todd was dead.

Then from shock or fever or worry or grief or all of them together, Dolly also became very sick. At the same time, and while Dolly lay almost unconscious, the new baby caught the fever. The baby had no strength against the disease, and he died. Dolly fought for her life. After a long fight, and very, very slowly, she recovered.

In November, the women and Dolly's first-born, Payne Todd, made their sad return to the city. Others were straggling back as well. There were friends to greet and friends and family to be mourned. There were neglected houses to be put in order. There were all the things of daily living which needed attention. For Dolly, there was a little boy to tend. There was now also Dolly's younger sister, Anna, who came to live with her.

There was so much to be done that Dolly simply could not be idle. Besides, no one was around to help her but herself. She was young and had courage. She took up her life again, quietly, but with strength.

4. JEMMY

ONE of Dolly's best friends through all
her life was a woman of her own age
named Elizabeth Collins, who later
became Mrs. Lee. Elizabeth was a Quaker and
a Philadelphian. She had been a witness at
Dolly's wedding to John Todd. She would live
to attend Dolly's funeral fifty-nine years after
that wedding. She loved Dolly and she was
amused by her, particularly by her prettiness
and her attraction for men.

Elizabeth Collins once said of Dolly that
"gentlemen would station themselves where
they could see her pass." And to Dolly she
gave the half-laughing advice, "Really Dolly,
thou must hide thy face, there are so many
staring at thee."

But Dolly did not hide her face. She felt
she had nothing to hide. She did not bid for
attention. Attention came to her. She knew

that a young woman was not expected to remain a widow forever. But she was in no
hurry to remarry. She had been happy with
her first husband. If she married again, it
would be because she expected to be happy
with her second husband. She had a great deal
of affection and warmth to give, but she did
not intend to give it just anywhere at all. She
made friends with some men, among them
Aaron Burr, who had been a boarder at her
mother's house.

Aaron Burr was a charmer. He said of himself, "It seems I must move always in a whirl-
wind." He was thriftless and impulsive and
impractical. He was wrong as often, if not
oftener, than he was right, but he was quick-
witted and attractive. And he was one of the
few men of his day who believed that women
had minds equal to men's and who thought
that these minds should be trained equally
with men's. He enjoyed female society. Although he did not pay court to Dolly, he admired her and was very friendly with her.

One spring day in 1794, perhaps the most
important day in her life, she received a note
from Aaron Burr.

She tried to take the news in the note
calmly, but the message she immediately wrote

to her friend, Elizabeth Collins, gives her away. She was not calm at all. "Dear Friend," she wrote, "Thou must come to me. Aaron Burr says that the 'great little Madison' has asked to be brought to see me this evening."

"The great little Madison" was not Dolly's special name for this man. He was called that quite generally. He was great, and he was little. He was shorter than the average man, and his figure was slight. But his proportions were good, and his fine head and face gave him distinction. The animation in his eyes showed his friendliness and his intelligence. He was forty-three years old at the time he first came to call on Dolly Payne Todd, but he had already done enough and learned enough and taught enough for most men of ninety.

In a day in the United States when colleges were rare and scholars were rarer, James Madison had been a serious scholar and had graduated from what is now Princeton but was then called the College of New Jersey. He had gone there from his home in Virginia, where his parents, who had money and education themselves, had already given him the beginnings of a good education. His college studies included learning how governments of other times had been set up and how they had worked. At college, also, he had learned to think deeply and to express himself well. Then he had gone into politics.

As a member of the Virginia Convention of 1776, he had helped to draft that state's constitution. In the Continental Congress, during the Revolutionary War, he had caught the attention and won the respectful friendship of Thomas Jefferson, Benjamin Franklin and other leaders. While a delegate to the Constitutional Convention, he had recorded the proceedings. He had also had a tremendously important part in drafting the Constitution. He had greatly influenced his own state, Virginia, to ratify. He had written twenty-nine of the *Federalist* papers explaining the Constitution. It was Madison who had proposed the first ten constitutional amendments, the safeguards of civil liberties, known as the Bill of Rights.

He had shown himself to be ambitious, but with an ambition for matters far beyond self. He had proved that his ideals of government were based on solid, practical needs and that he had energy and patience, knowledge and ability. He was quiet, somewhat shy, but he was in no way stiff or cold. His friends had

34

given him the affectionate nickname, "Jemmy."

His request to be taken to call on a young woman was a very flattering thing indeed.

Dolly had heard, along with most other Philadelphians, that Madison had once been engaged to be married and that the engagement had been broken. But this had been quite a few years before. Madison had been living in a Philadelphia boarding house then and had become engaged to a girl who lived there with her father, another delegate to the Continental Congress. The engagement did not last long. The girl sent Madison a note one day, telling him that she was going to marry a minister. She returned the miniature of Madison which he had given her and asked that he return a similar picture of her. And then, either in insult or in carelessness, instead of using the usual sealing wax on her note, she sealed the letter with a piece of rye-bread dough.

Since that time, James Madison had not been known to pay special attention to any woman. But from the night of his first visit he began paying noticeable attention to Dolly.

That first evening Dolly wore her best dress. It was made of mulberry colored satin and

Madison's fiancée returned his miniature

had a silk tulle kerchief around the neck. On
her head she wore her filmiest, daintiest cap.
Her hair was dark against the white material;
her color was high and her eyes bright. In a
room where the fine furniture and the silver
gleamed and sparkled in candlelight, she must
have been a lovely sight as she rose to greet
and curtsy to her distinguished guests. With
her charm and her simplicity, her thoughtful-

ness and her buoyancy, she must have gotten the conversation off to an easy start.

Madison, described by Henry Adams as "quiet, somewhat precise in manner, pleasant, fond of conversation, with a certain mixture of ease and dignity in his address," was there to make the best impression he could. So he must have kept the talk going pleasantly and well.

In a few weeks, the rumor was going about that Madison and Dolly were engaged. The rumor was not true, but apparently people could feel what was coming.

Then Dolly received another note. This one was from Martha Washington, who asked Dolly to call at the nearby Presidential Mansion. Dolly pretended not to know why she was being sent for, but of course she went to call.

Soon she could not doubt the purpose of the summons, for Mrs. Washington said, "Dolly, is it true that you are engaged to James Madison?"

"No," Dolly said, "I think not."

Mrs. Washington was not convinced by the denial. "If it is so, do not be ashamed to confess it," she said. "Rather be proud. He will make thee a good husband, and all the better for being so much older. We both approve of it. The esteem and friendship existing between Mr. Madison and my husband is very great, and we would wish thee to be happy."

But Dolly was going to make up her own mind. She was not going to let even the President's wife tell her what to do. She knew, by now, that Madison wanted her to marry him, but she needed time to think it over. She preferred to consider all sides of the question. She felt that Madison, for all his reserve and modesty, was well aware of his talents and duties. He would probably spend much of his life as a public man. The wife of such a man could not lead the quiet life she had been leading, but instead would be in the midst of strenuous, exciting events and would have much hard work. If she married a non-Quaker she could not continue in the meeting and little Payne would be brought up in a way quite different from the Quaker way. She knew that Madison was as gentle and considerate as her first husband had been. She had discovered that James was a profound thinker, much more profound than she could ever hope to be. She wondered if she could possibly live up to all that would be expected of her. She wondered if he was too serious for her or too old. But she was sure that he loved her, tenderly and respectfully.

To give herself a chance to know her true feelings, Dolly took a trip by stagecoach to Virginia. Payne and her sister, Anna, bounced over the rough roads and forded the rivers with her. Madison, at the same time, traveled to his home, Montpelier, in Orange County, Virginia. There was no one close by to influence Dolly. She could decide for herself.

She did. She suddenly wrote to Madison at Montpelier that she would marry him.

On August 18, 1794, he sent her a joyous, almost worshipful reply. "I received some days ago your precious favor. . . . I cannot express, but hope you will conceive, the joy it gave me. . . . I hope you will never have another deliberation on that subject. If the sentiments of my heart can guarantee those of yours, they assure me there can never be a cause for it."

Dolly's "deliberation on that subject" was written by her on her wedding day to her friend, Elizabeth Collins. "I give my hand to the man who of all others I most admire."

5. POLITICS AND PARTIES

THE wedding of James and Dolly Madison took place in September at Harewood in Virginia. Harewood was the home of Dolly's younger sister, Lucy, and President Washington's nephew, George Steptoe Washington. It was a stately colonial house with paneled rooms and a fine fluted stairway. It made a gracious, friendly setting for a wedding. Dolly's mother and son and sisters were there among the lively, merrymaking guests.

Around Dolly's neck was a necklace of medallions in mosaic work, each medallion made from tiny bits of carved and fitted colored stone. This was what James, her "Jemmy," had given her as a wedding gift. But Jemmy's clothes, for once, created more interest than Dolly's. Usually the little man was plainly dressed. But today, to match the glowing hap-

Lady guests cut up Madison's flowing ruffles

piness in his face, he was resplendent in silken coat, knee breeches and a shirt ruffled with fine Mechlin lace. After the ceremony the young lady guests scurried around souvenir hunting, cutting up his flowing ruffles and snatching pieces of them as keepsakes. Perhaps they merely wanted a wedding remembrance. But perhaps, on the other hand, they felt that here was a famous man and one whom time would make more famous.

They had reason to think so. For James Madison was becoming more prominent year by year. He was taking his public duties very, very seriously. Although he was in love and wanted to have time alone with his wife at Montpelier, although he was proud of her and wanted to show her off to his parents there, he did neither of these things.

Instead he and Dolly stayed a few days at Harewood and then piled their horsehair trunks into a coach and started off. They broke the journey by a brief visit to Madison's sister. Then they returned to Philadelphia and to James's work as a member of Congress.

They returned to political uproar.

Five years before this, in 1789, at the very start of Washington's first administration, disagreement had begun about the actual meaning of the Constitution of the new United States. It was not enough to have ratified a constitution. The people and the Congress and the Cabinet next had to decide just exactly what the Constitution said or allowed.

Thomas Jefferson was Secretary of State in Washington's first administration, and Alexander Hamilton was Secretary of the Treasury. And the country began to divide into two opposing parties around the ideas of these two men. Jefferson's party was the Democratic-Republican. Hamilton's party was the Federalist. Jefferson's party believed in the strictest construction or following of the Constitution; Hamilton's party did not. James Madison, as soon as the Constitution was ratified, believed in following it strictly, too. He became anti-Federalist, and was the leader, in Congress, of Jefferson's Democratic-Republican party.

Hamilton was emphatically in favor of a strong national government. He also felt that the wealthy people of the country should be a kind of ruling class. He stated clearly that he did not think the voice of the people was the voice of God. Jefferson, of course, debated hotly with him. For Jefferson believed in states' rights and that the people, rich or poor, in cities or in the country, could be left to govern themselves through their representatives. Madison differed from both these men. But he sided with Jefferson, taking some of Jefferson's vision and theories, and working them out in ways that were practical and safe. Eventually the country could take the differing aims of Hamilton and Jefferson, the aims of efficiency as opposed to personal liberty, and mold them together for the country's good. But that could not happen at once.

Some three years before Madison and Dolly were married, the political parties split far apart on the questions of debts owed by the states from the Revolutionary War, on taxes, and on a national bank. Hamilton won a large part of this round when President Washington signed a bill to charter a national bank. But a compromise was necessary on the debt question. The New England states, with Hamilton leading them, wanted the new Federal government to take over the state debts. The Southern states, led by Madison, opposed this. On the other hand, the Southern states wanted a Federal capital along the Potomac. The New Englanders preferred Philadelphia as the capital city. Madison and Hamilton finally agreed on a compromise. The debts were taken over by the Federal government, and a new national capital was planned in a ten-mile area to be known as the District of Columbia. Philadelphia would remain the capital while the new Federal City was being built.

By the time of the Madisons' marriage, Jefferson had resigned as Secretary of State. But the differences of the two parties were still very strong. Just after James and Dolly returned to Philadelphia, much of the storm broke out around the "Jay Treaty." This was an agreement arranged by John Jay between the United States and England.

Jay was a Federalist, but he was criticized because his treaty permitted England to say that American cotton should not be exported in American ships. The rest of the agreement, which was supposed to have settled questions left over from the Revolutionary War, seemed to many of its opponents just as weak. Jefferson's followers got excited enough to burn Jay in effigy, but Washington signed the treaty none the less. And Andrew Jackson got excited enough by this signing to say that Washington should be impeached for it.

So Dolly, with Madison as her husband, was thrown at once into the midst of the greatest political debate. Whenever the Madisons went out, people were discussing both sides. At their Philadelphia home, too, they heard both sides because they invited people of differing opinions to their dinners. Dolly did not then, or ever, try to take an active part in politics. But just getting these people together had a political effect. The guests, enjoying good food and wine, enjoying a comfortable, hospitable atmosphere, found their differences becoming more reasonable and less personal. The government men and their wives, as well as the

foreigners in America on official business, re-
laxing with one another, felt a beginning of
harmony. The fact that their host was one of
the most balanced and learned men of the day
and that their hostess knew when to keep
silent and when to encourage talk, helped to
make the Madison dinner parties interesting
and valuable.

Almost at once, Dolly began to be known
as a good hostess. She did not particularly try
for the reputation. She simply enjoyed giving
parties. If most of the entertaining had a political side, that was quite agreeable to her. If
some of it was purely social, she was pleased
by that also.

Soon she found that as hostess in this new
circle she could and should begin to dress up.
She loved that, too. But in liking clothes and
finery, she was not terribly different from the
women around her. She was different only in
seeming to have a natural sense of what
looked best on her. It was not just natural,
though, but was a result of the wide-eyed
study of beautiful women which she had begun as a girl of fifteen.

Philadelphia at this time was a gay and
dressy place. The women pored over fashion
magazines. They went to see dolls which had

been shipped from England to show the latest styles in that country. They begged their friends who were going to France to write them fashion news and to buy a hat or dress or ornament for them in Paris so that they would have the newest and most fashionable things. They wrote each other long letters from city to city in America on what they had worn or what they had seen other women wearing at receptions and teas and balls. They cherished their fine silks and brocades, their ruffles and flounces, their laces and feathers, their hats, their snuffboxes, their reticules, their colored kid slippers.

It was not at all queer, either, for a Quaker at this period to be interested in clothes and to be wearing lively colors and rich materials. Ways were changing. And while Quaker women would not dress as lavishly or as brightly as others, they sometimes broke away from their severe plain grays. Dolly had done nothing unusual, for the times, to wear mulberry satin when she first received James Madison. But the clothes and ornaments which she wore after her marriage to him were far more elaborate than even the changing Quakers thought fitting.

Once when she was wearing a bare-shoul-

Philadelphia women studying English fashion

dered evening dress, she teased a hatless
Quaker friend of hers with the toast, "Here's
to thy absent broadbrim, Friend Hallowell."
The man quickly raised his wine glass to hers,
bowed and said, "And here's to thy absent
kerchief, Friend Dorothy."

She was, of course, entirely within her
rights in dressing any way she pleased. For
just as Dolly's father had been "read out of

meeting" for bankruptcy, so was Dolly disowned by the Society of Friends for marrying Madison who was not a Quaker.

She still wore her Quaker clothes for morning use at home. And she kept to the Quaker character of simplicity and plainness in all her ways and all her dealings with people. But her new elegance in social dress seemed to give her new assurance and to help bring out characteristics in her which had not had much chance to show themselves before. She was lively, witty, talkative. She had always been friendly; now she was friendly with more people. She had always been curious and eager; now she was curious and eager about more things.

The entertaining had something else to it that she enjoyed. Her marriage was turning out even better than she had hoped. And as she grew more and more fond of Jemmy, it was a pleasure to succeed at giving these parties where he could broaden his political circle and move freely with people who would be important to him and his causes. He might sometimes remain quiet and a little aloof. But he could also have fun, and he was obviously happy when Dolly was entertaining.

49

Dolly was sure that James would never be the butterfly she was, but she could see that he enjoyed watching her develop under a new kind of experience and a new way of living.

6. VIRGINIA INTERLUDE

"AFTER a warm contest for the succession to General Washington, the vacancy will be filled by Mr. Adams. He has seventy-one votes, and Mr. Jefferson only sixty-eight. . . . Mr. Jefferson, it is now well known, will serve in the secondary place allotted to him. This being the last session of Congress of which I shall be a member, I must, at the same time that I return you thanks for all your past favors, request that your future ones be addressed to Orange County, Virginia."

The writer of this letter was James Madison. The time of its writing was after George Washington had refused to run for a third term and was preparing his Farewell Address. Although James's letter does not mention the Farewell, he had a special personal interest in it. For at the end of Washington's first term, he had asked Madison to write a farewell address for him. That was before Washington knew that the public and public affairs would force him to accept office again. But when Washington had found he must serve once more, he had set Madison's draft aside. Now, however, the outgoing President had recovered it. Using Madison's words as a basis, he wrote his famous message, explaining why he would not run for a third term, how the people of America should preserve their new government, how much they needed education, religion and good faith, and what they should do in relation to other nations. For final revisions he submitted his paper to Hamilton.

It seems from the name "Farewell Address" that this must have been a speech delivered to the public, but it was not. Dolly and James did not hear it. Like everyone else, they read it in a Philadelphia newspaper. However, like others in Philadelphia, they were able to see Washington making his farewell appearances.

Washington's black velvet suit, the dress sword hanging in its green scabbard, the diamond knee buckles, the snowy ruffled shirt and the snowy wig were familiar sights. He was a tall, erect, noble-looking, ruddy-faced man. Now in his middle sixties, he had been their wartime and their peacetime leader for

*A crowd watched Washington leave the
Presidential Mansion*

twenty years. As he bowed out for the new
President, they knew sadly that they were saying good-bye to someone who had been strong
and vital in their lives. A crowd followed
Washington when he went to Adams' house
to pay his respects. It was an "immense company, going as one man in total silence, his
escort all the way."

Later, on March ninth, another saddened crowd gathered for a last view of the heavy Washington coach. It was a pale cream color, crested with the family coat of arms and drawn by six fine horses. The citizens stood, silent again, as George and Martha Washington came out of the Presidential Mansion and entered this coach for a final journey to Mount Vernon.

Meanwhile, in those days just before Washington's departure, the Madisons and other people were also watching the new President, pudgy, fiery-tempered John Adams. For eight years he had been Vice-President. And while he had managed to quarrel with almost everyone in government, he had said that the position of Vice-President was "the most insignificant office that ever the invention of man contrived or his imagination conceived." Dolly and James had great curiosity as to what things would be like with Adams as President and with their good friend Jefferson, to whom no job could ever seem insignificant, the new Vice-President.

They had even greater curiosity as to what their own life would be, now that Madison had retired from Congress. They were free to pack their belongings, say good-bye to their friends, climb into their coach and head south for Montpelier.

Madison, as well as Dolly, had two ways of looking at his activities. He enjoyed being in the political thick of things. He enjoyed mental struggle, debate, decision. But, while busiest with affairs of government, he always held the hope that he could eventually retire to Orange County and become a gentleman farmer for the rest of his days. He knew he was too involved in the political life of the nation for this to be wholly possible. But, at least while Adams was in office, the wish could be partly realized.

Madison was glad just to return to the soil of Montpelier. He loved that deep red clay and the feeling of the abundance of nature about him, the distant hazy Blue Ridge Mountains, the flourishing fields of tobacco, wheat and corn, the grazing cattle and the forests of virgin timber. His chief source of income was here. He knew he must keep in close touch with the place always and make the most he could out of it. Yet even though he worked hard at Montpelier, he looked better and felt healthier than he had for a long time.

For Dolly, too, the change was beneficial. Here in her gardens she could indulge her love of flowers and plants. Here in orchard and field and woods she delighted in the peach blossoms and clover, redbud and dogwood. James was having the stately, porticoed, red brick house remodeled so that his parents as well as he and Dolly could live there comfortably. Here Dolly could help create order and grace.

Perhaps her only mistake, and it was a mistake she made when she lived other places also, was that of being too indulgent to Payne. She loved the little boy. He was her one child, for she and Madison had had none together. Madison apparently loved him, too. He accepted Payne as his own and did everything for him he would have done for his own. Like Dolly, he never refused him anything. Dolly did not worry about this at the time, but when Payne was older and brought troubles to her, she must certainly have looked back to the earlier days and wondered.

She did not spoil her sister, Anna, the one she called "my sister-child," but she was extremely good to her. Anna, growing up, lived the full life of the Madisons. She shared all the contentment of Montpelier with them.

One of the very happy things at Montpelier was Dolly's discovery that James's feeling

56

*Jefferson enjoyed showing off his home,
Monticello*

about slaves was much the same as hers. The
Madison family owned many. Madison did not
free them, as Dolly's father had, but he treated
them like people and he would not sell them.
He had grown up with slaves. When he was
a child, he had played mostly with slave children. As a man, he followed the thinking of

other Virginia gentlemen and considered slaves his servants. Yet he acted toward them with the kindness and helpfulness of a parent.

Another pleasant thing for Dolly at Montpelier was that Thomas Jefferson was a neighbor. His home, Monticello, was not too many miles away. In the summers when he came back to Virginia, visits were exchanged frequently. There were extraordinary things to see at Monticello and tall, lanky, sandy-haired Jefferson took great pleasure in showing them off. He had been architect, builder and decorator for this home. He was also the inventor of its numerous gadgets: a clock which showed the days of the week and which had two faces so that people could read the time inside or outside of the house, a folding ladder for climbing up to wind the clock, a dumbwaiter hidden in his dining-room mantel so that wines could be brought up easily from the basement. His bed, on pulleys, could be raised out of his way in the daytime. He had several adjustable tables and the first swivel chair. In addition to all the things already perfected, he was forever thinking of new inventions and talking them over with his friends.

Dolly discovered that Jefferson and her

Jemmy had many, many things in common. She had known how well they fitted together politically and how each respected and admired the other. Now she had a chance to learn of their shared interest in reading and study, in the out-of-doors, in watching even the smallest creatures of nature, in riding horseback over the hills. She listened while they discussed their tobacco crops and prices, the purchase of horses or cattle. She listened particularly when they discussed the new capital city being built on the Potomac.

Even here in the Virginia hills, the thought of that new city fascinated her. Jefferson's enthusiastic description of the plan of the city and the details of the future buildings excited and intrigued her more than they did James. She tried to picture it all in her mind. She wondered when and if she would see this District of Columbia. She knew that Jefferson liked her, but she did not know how often he had observed her as she smiled and chatted, fitting in with any group, being the same to all kinds of people. She did not know how often other observers had talked to him of these traits in her. She could not possibly guess how much he admired all this nor how greatly he would later depend on her as a friend, as a helper and as a hostess in that new Federal City called Washington.

Dolly could not even faintly dream of the years that would follow Jefferson's time in Washington nor in any way imagine her own immense part in those years.

7. THE FEDERAL CITY

THE Indian name for the Potomac River was a prophetic one. They called it Potowmak, the river of the meeting of the tribes. In 1788, ten square miles of land adjoining this river was ceded by the state of Maryland to Congress, and Congress accepted it as a site for a Federal city. People approved because the location was so *central*. At that time the future District of Columbia and city of Washington were nearly in the heart of the United States.

The exact spot on which the city was to be built was left to the discretion of President Washington. He had been a surveyor in his youth and now accompanied the first surveying party above tidewater on the Potomac. They traveled in a piroque or canoe, "hollowed out of a great poplar tree, hauled on a wagon to the bank and there launched."

This surveying craft was no more primitive than everything else about the new city. There was little to begin with except farm land and swamp land and forest. Washington engaged an architect and engineer, Major Pierre Charles L'Enfant, to lay out a city plan. L'Enfant rode over the ground on horseback, looking and thinking, and then made an enthusiastic report to the President on the possibilities of this place. Where L'Enfant found a thickly forested hill, his imagination transformed it, and he called it "a pedestal waiting for a monument." This was the site he chose for the Capitol building. From this site, he planned the principal avenues to radiate out like the spokes of a wheel. Other wide, tree-lined streets were to run perpendicular to the avenues.

All of his design had symmetry and majesty. The final development of the city largely followed his plan, but L'Enfant's personality was not fitted to cooperation. He fought with the commissioners. He lawlessly destroyed a house which was being built where he proposed to have a street. He would not let his plans be publicly inspected so that people could buy lots. It became necessary to have someone else take over his job.

L'Enfant protested his loss of this position for the rest of his life. For years, the tall thin man in a high-buttoned blue military coat, walked around the city day after day, carrying a roll of papers which were his supposed claim upon the government. Some even say that at the moment he died he was clutching a plan of the city of Washington to his breast.

Three men, Hallet, Dr. Thornton and La-Trobe, all had a part in the design of the Capitol building. But most of the Capitol as it was originally built was the work of the one of them who was actually neither a professional architect nor engineer. This was Dr. Thornton. He had had training as a doctor of medicine. He was also a scholar, a poet and an inventor. He was very, very valuable to the new city as a commissioner, and he and his wife became great friends of the Madisons.

The house where the Presidents would live was the work of the architect, James Hoban, an Irishman. He had won the right to build it in a public competition. This house was one destined for many alterations, but since the core of it was sound and its proportions had simple dignity, it could cast off the poor alterations and keep the good ones. The long two-storied house was built of gray stone. It had a balustrade around the roof, and although it had no porticoes to begin with, there were tall stone pillars at the entrance. In the size and grandeur of the exterior, there was also a feeling of a nation not afraid to build in a wilderness, a nation that would be permanent.

*Major L'Enfant walked around Washington
day after day*

As the new city rose, most of the people in Washington also became amateur architects, at least in words of approval or disapproval of plans. Washington, until his death in 1799, and Jefferson, even after that, had their fingers in every pie. Lesser men spoke out and were listened to. It was everybody's project.

Yet in spite of all the interest, the work went along very slowly. Ten years after the land had been set aside, a small "packet sloop" sailed from Philadelphia. It carried the state papers and furniture, all the movable possessions of the young Republic to the new home of that Republic. People watched these things being unloaded on a dock and then carried by wagon to the Capitol building. Some observers said, "Pennsylvania Avenue . . . from the Capitol to the Presidential Mansion, was nearly the whole distance, a deep morass covered with alder bushes." One of the observers, Gouverneur Morris said sarcastically, "We want nothing here but houses, cellars, kitchens, well-informed men, amiable women and other trifles of this kind to make our city perfect. . . . In short, it is the very best city in the world for a future residence."

The first President to take up residence in Washington did not want to go there. He,

John Adams, still thought Philadelphia a much better place, and that the new Federal City was a wasteland. His wife Abigail agreed with him. She wrote to her daughter (November 27, 1800):

"The vessel which has my clothes and other matters is not arrived. The ladies are impatient for a drawing room. I have no looking glasses but dwarfs for this house, nor a twentieth part lamps enough to light it. . . . My rooms are very pleasant and warm whilst the doors of the hall are closed. You can scarcely believe that here in this wilderness city I should find my time so occupied as it is. My visitors come some of them three or four miles. To return one of them is the work of a day. Mrs. Otis, my nearest neighbor, is at lodgings almost half a mile from me; Mrs. Senator Otis, two miles. We have all been very well as yet. If we can, by any means, get wood, we shall not let our fires go out, but it is at a price indeed; from four dollars it has risen to nine. Some say it will fall, but there must be more industry than is to be found here to bring half enough to the market for the consumption of the inhabitants."

And of her arrival in the city Mrs. Adams also wrote:

"Woods are all you see from Baltimore un-

66

til you reach the city which is only in name. Here and there is a small hut, without a glass window, interspersed amongst the forests, through which you travel miles without seeing any human being."

She writes then of the President's House, of how huge and incomplete and hard to keep up it is, and she adds:

"there is not a single apartment finished. . . . We have not the least fence, yard or convenience without, and the great unfinished audience room I make a drying room of, to hang up the clothes in."

Although Adams is known to have been unhappy with the new city and although he was usually a rather stern, formal kind of man, there is one story that shows him to have been as much the pioneer in Washington as anyone else. The Treasury Office on F Street caught fire, and a fire brigade formed to put it out. Men stood in line, handing buckets of water to one another so that water could get from its source to the fire. Adams walked by, saw the fire and without any thought of his rank, joined the line passing buckets to and from the burning building. It was not until others insisted that the day was cold and damp and that a President must not take chances with his health, that he was persuaded to stop.

Mrs. Adams did not have to put up with the discomforts of the new city and the President's Palace for long, for Adams was defeated in the election a month after the capital moved

President Adams joined the bucket brigade

to Washington. And a new President took over three months after that. It is characteristic of Mrs. Adams, however, that she called the President's House, our White House, a "palace." Her husband had wanted George Washington to be called "His Highness," and

Abigail had felt that the office of President should receive almost royal honors. She had approved of Washington's crests, the red carpets that were unrolled for him, the princely way he received at his "levees." She favored as much ceremony as possible for herself and her husband. And at her New Year's Day reception, in 1801, the first official reception ever held in the President's Palace, she showed that she felt this way.

Dolly and James were not at this reception. They were still living at Montpelier. But they knew now that the chances were that they would soon return to political life.

The election in the December just past had been between the Federalists, Adams and Pinckney, and the Democratic-Republicans, Jefferson and Aaron Burr. The Federalists had lost; the Democratic-Republicans were in. But the presidency was not yet decided because there was a tie between Jefferson and Burr. Without a tie, the one who had received the most votes would automatically have been the President; the one who received the second highest number, the Vice-President. With a tie, the election had to be decided by the House of Representatives, a body now representing sixteen states since Vermont, Kentucky and Tennessee had joined the Union.

Dolly and James awaited the news of this balloting tensely and eagerly. They were unable to leave Montpelier just then because Madison's father was dying. But even if they had been in Washington, they would not have known how the representatives were voting unless Madison had been one of them. The vote was secret. All that was known outside Sutter's Tavern where they voted, was that there was a deadlock for nearly a week. Finally, after thirty-six ballots, the deadlock was broken. Jefferson was President. Aaron Burr was Vice-President. And James Madison would soon be appointed by Jefferson to that superior office, Secretary of State.

In Baltimore, Philadelphia and New York, cannon were fired when news came that Jefferson was President. But Adams was not pleased. On March 4, 1801, the first inaugural day in the city of Washington, Adams did not go to the Senate when Jefferson took the oath of office nor to the reception at Jefferson's lodgings. He said he was unwilling "to act the role of captive-chief in the triumphant procession of the victor to the Capitol." He rudely left the city without seeing the incoming President.

This lack of ceremony did not bother or offend Jefferson. He felt there had been too much ceremony in the administrations of Washington and Adams, and he immediately began to make changes. He would not tell the date of his own birthday lest the birthday be celebrated, would not, on any day, have receptions imitating royalty. Nor would he allow anybody to call him by any kind of title. He had always dressed simply, almost sloppily, and he refused to change his way of dress. He continued, for example, to wear leather thongs when others were wearing fancy silver shoe buckles. He had always moved about independently and without pomp, and he insisted on still doing so. Although men of less importance than he drove about in a coach and four, he went almost everywhere on horseback.

But after he had been in Washington for just a little while, he began to see that simplicity was not enough. There were some social affairs that needed more handling than a widower President could give them. There were some social affairs that could be simple but that still needed a woman's touch. He knew where to look for the woman to give the touch.

A GREAT-NIECE of Dolly Madison once said that Dolly had "a willingness to be pleased." This willingness proved a most valuable trait, both to herself and those around her, when Dolly first moved to Washington in May, 1801.

The great Federal City was still a village of scattered one-, two- and three-story houses, some frame, some brick. Muddy roads and unhealthy swamp vapors prevailed. There were more forests than buildings, more fields than fences. There was a grocery store in a small brick house, a dry goods store in a two-story frame one, a tavern in another two-story house. The famous Sutter's Tavern was a one-story frame building. There were some public buildings nearly finished; there were others in "a state of advancement." There was a cabinet-maker, a saddler, some brick makers, a stonecutter, a milliner, a soap maker and chandler, a bookbinder, a tailor, a coach maker, an auction store, a bake house. There was a market to which country people brought their produce on horseback and to which tobacco was brought in huge hogsheads, fitted out with axle and shaft and pulled by a horse. There were the "Six Buildings" and "Seven Buildings," two groups of houses tightly set together. There were numerous boarding houses.

To those who did not have "a willingness to be pleased" there was still much to criticize. Oliver Wolcott, Secretary of the Treasury, wrote his wife:

> "The President's house was built to be looked at by visitors and strangers, and will render its occupant an object of ridicule with some, and of pity with others. It must be cold and damp in winter and cannot be kept in tolerable order without a regiment of servants.
>
> "The Capitol is situated on an eminence, which I should suppose was near the center of the city. It is a mile and a half from the President's house. There is one good tavern about forty rods from the Capitol, and several other houses are built or erecting, but I do not perceive how the members of Congress can possibly secure lodgings unless they will

consent to live like scholars in a college or monks in a monastery, crowded twenty in one house and utterly excluded from society."

And even some who could not help admiring the Presidential Mansion had to find ways to object to it:

"The President's house, a very noble structure, is by no means suited to the philosophical humility of its present possessor (Jefferson) who inhabits but a corner of the mansion itself. . . . This grand edifice is encircled by a very rude pale (a crude fence), through which a common rustic stile introduces the visitors to the first man in America."

But Dolly, always intrigued by change and progress, found the President's Mansion fascinating and the ways of the new President very exciting. Jefferson stayed firm in his resolution not to let the presidency become kingly, yet he made the President's House comfortable and elegant. From the first, he had been interested in Hoban's design for the house. With Benjamin LaTrobe, he helped plan additions to it. He brought his slaves from Monticello and sent for cartloads of furniture from there. In furnishing twenty-three of the rooms, he purchased beautiful chintz curtains, Brussels

The Presidential Mansion was encircled by a crude fence

carpets and the fashionable painted-canvas floor coverings. Because he was still fond of invention and convenience, he devised new sets of revolving shelves from pantry to dining room and a revolving cupboard for his clothes.

Dolly and James did not have a home waiting for them in Washington, so they stayed for a few weeks with Jefferson in the President's House. Eventually, though, they moved into a small, newly finished, rented house. They immediately took the newness and rawness of the Federal City as a kind of challenge.

76

The inconveniences were something to ignore or improve upon; the hazards were something to brave or do away with; the beauties were to enjoy. They began to entertain, officially as Secretary of State and wife, unofficially as the Madisons.

Their invitations to official parties were for the season, to members of Congress, the heads of departments, the foreign ministers, and to particular friends. The Secretary of State and Mrs. Madison would "earnestly request the pleasure" of someone's company for a series of receptions to be given, say, every other Wednesday while Congress was in session. The guests would arrive about eight o'clock in their private carriages or in public hacks. The conveyances would wait, ranged along the street, until the party was over. The guests, dressed almost as if for a ball, would bow to the host and hostess, dance, play cards, eat, chat, and would leave at about ten.

The unofficial parties were, of course, smaller, and were more often dinners than receptions. These also ended by ten, but they began at the usual dinner hour of about four in the afternoon. Dolly's dinners immediately became famous for the wonderful food she served. But all her parties became famous for the abundance of her own good nature, her generosity and tact.

At one of her receptions, Dolly looked around as she generally did to see how each of her guests was getting along. She noticed that a very bashful young man had flattened himself against a wall and that he stood there in terror, unable to move, unable to talk to anyone. After he had been half an hour in this position, Dolly saw him relax just enough to be able to accept and drink a cup of coffee when it was passed. In pity she walked across the room to talk to him. But her approach increased his shyness so much that he dropped the saucer onto the floor and stuffed the empty cup into his pocket. Dolly pretended for his sake that someone had bumped into him. "The crowd is so great that no one can avoid being jostled," she said gently. "The servant will bring you another cup of coffee." Then she ignored his embarrassment altogether and asked him about his mother whom she remembered from a long-ago meeting. Soon the boy began to smile and move. He did not think of Dolly as sensitive or tactful. He merely knew that he, too, could talk about his mother and that a famous lady was as natural and homey as anyone he had ever met. After a while he was even able to take the cup from his pocket and return it to the table.

Someone else had seen the whole episode, and the story was repeated around Washington to become part of a growing legend about Dolly. For an amazing thing had begun to happen almost as soon as Dolly moved to the new capital, and it continued to happen throughout her years there. Everything she did was noticed. No one could ever say exactly why this was so except that there was apparently some spark of personality which set Dolly apart from everyone else. She was neither outstandingly beautiful nor particularly brilliant. Yet her words were echoed. Her styles were copied. Her dresses and jewelry were described in other women's diaries and letters and in the letters of men, as well. The reports of her doings were read eagerly in the newspapers. Her guests were considered fortunate to be invited, and they frankly admitted that they came to her parties to look at her, to listen to her and to be able to talk about her the following day.

None of the talk was unpleasant gossip. It was all in answer to: "How did Mrs. Madison look? What did Mrs. Madison wear? Who were Mrs. Madison's guests? What did Mrs.

Madison serve?" The most unflattering criticism ever made of her was by a disgruntled British diplomat's wife who said that a meal at her house was "more like a harvest home supper" than the stiff, state dinner it might have been. But Dolly's answer was typical. "The profusion of my table so repugnant to foreign customs arises from the happy circumstance of abundance and prosperity in our country."

Once in a while a story would be told that was almost too good to be true. One of these was that Henry Clay, who had not yet met her, came to the Madison house to call on James. Dolly answered the door and smiled at him so engagingly that Clay, having no idea who she was, kissed her. Just then Madison came toward the door, and Dolly kissed her husband. The astonished Clay said, "Had I, Madam, known you were Mrs. Madison the coin (the kiss) would have been larger."

Another later story of Dolly and this same Henry Clay was that he remarked to her, "Everybody loves Mrs. Madison" and that she replied, "Mrs. Madison loves everybody."

Dolly was also watched and talked about and imitated even when she was only paying or receiving morning visits. One early resident of the city said, "Morning seems to continue until dinner time," because the hours for these calls were from twelve noon until three o'clock. The official ladies of Washington made a ritual of calling. They would sit back in their gleaming carriages and direct their coachmen to take them from one house to another. Like Dolly, they might indulge in a pinch of snuff now and then while they were on the way. Like her, they would remain sitting in their carriages when they reached a destination and would send the footman to ring the doorbell. If the lady they wished to call on was at home, they would go in. Otherwise they would open their dainty little card cases, take out a calling card and direct the footman to leave it at the door with a servant. All of them knew that any hostess might say she was out if she was busy or if she did not care to receive a particular visitor.

If the ladies wished to walk rather than ride when they paid their calls, at least two of them would go together, for they had been taught that "a genteel female is rarely to be seen walking out unattended."

For the Dancing Assembly and other balls, Dolly had some rules of behavior that were strictly her own. Most of the women danced, her sister Anna among them, but Dolly would not. Perhaps she remained too much the Quaker to learn dancing. Certainly the Quaker education left its mark on her. Once when she was ill and left Washington for a while, she wrote to Anna, "I have had a lecture . . . on seeing too much company, and it brought to mind the time when our society used to control me entirely, and debar me from so many advantages and pleasures; even now, I feel my ancient terror revive in great degree."

But no fright or conscience interfered with her liking for the splendid carriage the Madisons owned nor with her joy in the trim, rapid pair of horses which Jemmy, an expert on horses, had bought for her. Usually Anna was with her when she drove out. Both ladies wore the latest fashion, the high-waisted sheer dresses, the short jackets called spencers, and the distinctive, lavishly trimmed hats or bonnets. Dolly had grown plumper and was obviously older than Anna, but it was she more than her sister whom people noticed. Sometimes Payne was with them, a big, dark-eyed, handsome twelve-year-old, who enjoyed seeing the sights of Washington and enjoyed being stared at.

In November, the ladies were driven to the

horse races, holding parasols above their heads to protect themselves from the sun. The carriages took places at the fence around the track. Madison and the men of other families came on horseback in order to be able to move about more freely. There was visiting between the occupants of carriages, and there were visits from the gentlemen on horseback. But the interest and excitement of the crowd centered on the races themselves. Horses were vital to these people for work and for transportation. If breeds could be improved through testing strength and endurance and speed, the people would benefit. If at the same time the spectators could wager and watch and cheer on a winner, so much the better.

Besides all the social diversion, there was naturally an extremely serious side to Washington life. Jefferson had many troubles, and Madison as Secretary of State shared most of them. Dolly, always sensitive and alert, knew when and how much he was troubled.

One of the first of the serious government problems was with the Barbary pirates, who pillaged ships and imprisoned sailors. Before the Revolution, the British had paid tribute to the Barbary States so that pirates from these North African countries would not interfere with shipping from America. The first two Presidents of the United States continued to do just what the British had done. Jefferson, though a notably peace-loving man, felt that resistance was necessary. He sent a squadron of warships to the North African waters. There were some battles, and he had a blockade set up. The United States was not yet strong enough to win against all four of the Barbary Coast countries, but Jefferson's blockade and battle ended with one of those countries signing a peace treaty favorable to the United States.

Far greater stress and tension for Jefferson's administration was set up through fears of what Napoleon might be planning to do. Napoleon's empire was growing. He had gained Louisiana from Spain in 1800. Now he was considering the possibility of extending his empire farther.

Neither Jefferson nor his advisers and cabinet liked the idea of Napoleon owning and ruling New Orleans. Thinking people easily understood why. Napoleon was too aggressive. There was no telling how far he might want to extend his powers. Jefferson and Madison also feared that the French in New Orleans might refuse to let the United States use the Mississippi River for shipping. And shipping along that river was becoming an increasing source of life, strength and income to the entire country.

Jefferson sent James Monroe to France as a special Minister to assist the other Minister, Robert Livingston. Their mission was to see if they could buy New Orleans and West Florida from the French. They had no idea what Napoleon's reaction would be to this offer, but they believed, rightly, that this was a good time to approach him. Just then Napoleon had enough to do, with a revolt of slaves in Haiti and with the possibility of another French war against England.

Apparently the timing was good. The negotiations ended with the United States buying the territory of Louisiana, in 1803, for the unbelievably small sum of fifteen million dollars. Suddenly, almost without warning, the United States was twice as big as it had been before.

The news of the purchase reached the capital the night before the Fourth of July, so the Fourth was celebrated with tremendous enthusiasm. "At an early hour the city was alive," says Samuel Smith, publisher of the newspaper, the *National Intelligencer*, "a discharge of 18

85

guns saluted the dawn, the military assembled exhibiting a martial appearance, at 11 o'clock an oration . . . at 12 company began to assemble at the President's . . . more numerous than I have before marked . . . enlivened too by the presence of between 40 and 50 ladies clothed in their best attire, cakes, punch, wine &c in profusion."

Still the purchase brought new troubles to the administration. Not everyone rejoiced that this vast area had been added to the country. The Federalists denounced the purchase as unconstitutional. There was ill-feeling and struggle before Congress approved.

Time won out though—time and visible results. In the end, everyone agreed that, in buying this land, Secretary of State Madison and President Jefferson had brought off a master stroke.

9. MRS. SECRETARY OF STATE

WHILE Secretary of State, Madison could be seen every morning quietly walking along from his house on F Street to the President's Mansion. He was dressed plainly, with his hair tied in a simple queue. (A Washington barber, whose livelihood depended on the use of wigs, powdered hair and long queues, complained of Madison: ". . . a queue no bigger than a pipe-stem. Sir, it is enough to make a man forswear his country.")

On many, many evenings, still looking slight and rather insignificant, still with the small queue, but a bit more dressed up, Madison could be seen being driven from F Street to the President's House. His Negro coachman and footman, Budin and Freeman, were on the box. Madison's wife, or perhaps his wife and his sister-in-law, were seated beside him in the carriage. The return to the President's Mansion in the evening would be because Dolly had received a letter like this:

"June 4, 1801. Thomas Jefferson was much disappointed at breakfast this morning, not having until then known of the departure of Mr. and Mrs. Madison and Miss Payne; he hopes they will come and dine today with the Miss Butters, who were assured they would meet them here, and tomorrow with Mrs. Gallatin and Mrs. Mason. Affectionate salutations."

Jefferson's dinners were for twelve or fourteen people and were informal and easy. Conversation was important to him, and he believed that a relaxed feeling on the part of the guests was a necessary spur to the conversation. He also believed that the hostess helped greatly to set the tone of the party. Occasionally, this widower President would have one of his two daughters staying with him to be his hostess. Once in a great while, he would call on some other Washington matron to help him out. But most of the time it was Dolly who would be summoned. And this was because she had proved to him, time and again, that she could make the evening a success.

Jefferson's requests for Dolly's time and

abilities were not, however, limited to asking her to "do the honors at the table." He asked her to be almost a mother to his daughters when they came to stay in the President's House. Although both of his daughters were married, neither one of them had had much experience in political social life. Both of them were simple and retiring. One of them was painfully shy. They did not know where or how to shop for the clothes and ornaments they would need for Washington gaieties, nor what would be their official duties and responsibilities. Dolly nestled them under her wing. She picked out hats and dresses and wigs for them. She coached them in the manners of the capital and in where and when to wear their finery. Jefferson left every choice to her discretion and would do no more than inquire of her "the amount, and the person" for whom things were bought.

Dolly herself had fun out of this. She had always loved shopping for herself. After she moved to Washington, she continued to buy many things in Philadelphia because there was more variety there. She had added to her pleasure by buying clothes for her sister, Anna. She saw that Madison himself had seemed to get pleasure out of providing the means whereby Anna could be as elegant as Dolly. And although it had been sad and painful for her when Anna married and moved away, Dolly had put enthusiasm and energy into buying the trousseau and giving the wedding. Now with Jefferson's daughters to outfit, she had a new and additional reason to visit all the shops, to study patterns of the beautiful, short-waisted empire dresses, to finger the rich fabrics, to debate over a turban or a feathered headdress. She was decidedly pleased. When she had finished her task, Jefferson and his daughters were pleased as well.

For a while, though, in 1804, just toward the end of Jefferson's administration, something happened to shock everyone into forgetfulness of fashion, visiting and shopping. The Vice-President of the United States shot and killed one of the noted citizens of the United States in a duel. It was Aaron Burr who killed Alexander Hamilton. Dueling was still fairly common, and many prominent men had fought their duels. But behind this particular challenge were years of political differences and much personal bad feeling. Many people believed that Hamilton fired into the air and

Aaron Burr killed Alexander Hamilton in a duel

that Burr had shot Hamilton down in cold
blood.

Burr was a complicated enough man to be
capable of anything. Gay, reckless and spend-
thrift, he could also burn with fierce anger
against even a political enemy. Though out-
wardly the two men had been friends, Burr
knew that Hamilton had helped defeat him

for the presidency when Jefferson was elected.
He knew also that Hamilton had a major part
in defeating him when Burr ran for Governor
of New York. He had seen a quotation from
one of Hamilton's letters which said that Burr
was "a dangerous man, and one who ought
not to be trusted with the reins of government." Burr had felt that a lifetime reputation
was at stake.

Hamilton was a complicated person, too.
He was a handsome, auburn-haired man with
lively brown eyes. He liked parties and good
conversation, but he was deadly serious when
it came to work. He was efficient, wanting
everything to be well-organized and being
able to organize everything he tried to do. He
also had a very quick temper and was inclined
to believe he was always right. Consequently
he got into many disastrous quarrels.

Two men with such temperaments could
readily provoke one another into a quarrel
fatal to one of them.

Although Burr survived and was unhurt
physically, the duel was, in another sense,
equally fatal to him. For he had proved that
Hamilton was right and that he was, indeed,
a dangerous man. The shooting was consid-

ered a scandal, and it was obvious that Aaron Burr's political career was ended.

Dolly had known Burr well and long and in many different guises, as the boarder in her mother's home, as the man who had introduced her to Madison, as the politician and statesman. She must have had many thoughts about him when she learned of the duel and its outcome. But she did not reveal any of them. A few months before the duel she had written to her sister on another subject, "I am learning to hold my tongue well." After the duel she wrote, "We go to Montpelier this week. Payne continues weak and sick, and my prospects rise and fall to sadness as this precious child recovers or declines. You have heard, no doubt, of the terrible duel and death of poor Hamilton." She certainly must have been tempted to say much more. But now, as well as on many occasions throughout her public life, Dolly was "brilliant in the things she did not say and do."

Within the next few years, she had a chance to hold back her words once more where Aaron Burr was concerned. For Burr had only begun to shock the nation. Some mad scheme came into his head; no one was ever sure ex-

actly what. It was either to start a separate
country of his own by taking the Western
states away from the United States or to start
a war of his own with Spanish Florida. Either
way, he was collecting soldiers and preparing
a secret military exploit when word of his
scheme came to the President. Jefferson immediately had him arrested and sent to Richmond to be tried for treason. In the end
Aaron Burr was acquitted, but at the time of
the trial the country rocked with talk about
him.

Dolly was so much the discreet wife of the
Secretary of State that, when she again wrote
to Anna, she merely said of this startling
affair, "I suppose you have heard that Burr
is retaken, and on his way to Richmond for
trial."

Her discretion showed up another time in
an entirely different circumstance. Madison
was in his drawing room entertaining a dele-
gation of Indians one evening, and Dolly was
upstairs in her bedroom. As she was undress-
ing, she looked in her mirror and could see
that an Indian in full war paint was hiding
behind her door. Indians at this time were
still apt to be cruelly savage, so besides being
startled, she was very frightened. But she

94

knew that if she screamed she would either be hurt or, almost worse, would insult and provoke to angry action the Indians sitting downstairs. So, mustering both brain and will power, she avoided looking toward the door. Instead she walked quietly into the next room where she could ring a bell for her maid. Then when the bell was answered, she and the servant walked with that same quietness back to the bedroom and gently persuaded the Indian to leave. No one downstairs was aware that anything unusual had happened to the wife of the Secretary of State. Not until long afterward did anyone hear the story. When people learned it, they added it to the legend of Dolly who could be cool for a purpose.

10. ENTER THE FIRST LADY

JEFFERSON would not run for a third term. Like Washington, he felt that he had devoted much of his life to his country. He wanted some years for himself and his own pursuits at Monticello. Madison, his trusted friend, helper and adviser with the "luminous and discriminating mind," seemed to him the best possible successor.

As the time for the nominations approached, Dolly could see which way the wind was blowing. She knew Jefferson's thoughts; she knew Madison's. She knew the party approved Jefferson's choice. She heard a great deal about the people's opinion of her husband.

She had been too much in and out of the President's Mansion, all during Jefferson's period there, to believe that being President meant only glamor, excitement and fun. She was sensitive enough to understand from what she had seen at close hand, that the highest position could hold weariness, worry and frightening responsibility. She was well aware that a man like Madison would bring to it devotion and dedication.

Although she undoubtedly had hours when she wished that Jemmy would turn back from it all, she kept quiet about it. As her great-niece said, she was "ambitious only that her husband's administration be a brilliant and successful one."

Even after Madison was elected, Dolly was not blind to what might be ahead. "I don't know that there is much cause for congratulation," she said. She looked at the willows planted at the side entrance of the President's House. "The President of the United States usually comes in at the iron gate and goes out at the weeping willows." No one knew better than Dolly that Jefferson's administration had left behind it crises which might well lead the new President "out at the weeping willows."

George Washington, in his Farewell Address, had said that because the United States was small and weak it must gain time "to settle and mature its yet recent institutions, and to progress without interruption to that degree of strength and consistency . . . necessary to

97

give it . . . the command of its own fortunes."

Jefferson shared this belief about gaining time to build strength. During his administration, he had tried many tactics to keep out of trouble with both France and England. Those countries were deep in war troubles with one another and were both trying to enlist friendly nations on their sides. Napoleon had all of Europe in turmoil. England seemed to be the only country with power to withstand him. England had a strong navy, France a strong army. The two countries issued various decrees against one another, each hoping to ruin the other's trade. France seized American merchandise. England, trying to become stronger than France, seized American sailors for England's navy. To the freedom-loving Americans this was an outrage, but England insisted on her "right of search" and the right of "impressment." American commerce suffered greatly, and American anger rose.

Then the commander of a United States frigate of thirty-six guns, the *Chesapeake*, refused to let a captain of a British ship, *Leopard*, search his vessel. The British opened fire and crippled the American ship.

Congress, in the hope of stopping further trouble, passed the Embargo Act. This said that American ships could not sail to foreign ports and foreign ships could not take exports from America. Immediately the Act began to ruin the commerce of New England and New York, so no one would abide by the embargo and it was soon repealed. In its place, Congress passed the Non-Intercourse Act. American ships could deal with all countries except France and Great Britain. Trade would be suspended with those two until they stopped violating the neutrality of the United States.

This was the situation when Madison came into office as President in 1809. None of it was new to him. As Secretary of State he had worked in extreme closeness with Jefferson for eight years. He had had his hand in the purchase of Louisiana and in the successful dealings with the Barbary pirates. He had taken part in all the ups and downs of the difficulties with France and England. He had negotiated continuously to defend the neutral rights of the United States and, at the same time, to keep out of war.

As he gave up his job of Secretary of State and took over the Presidency, he knew that criticism of two quite opposite kinds was waiting for him. Some called him a "warmonger"; others said he was going to have to be "kicked into war." The American people had not yet made up their minds that they wanted to fight. But they knew they were tired of having other countries take advantage of theirs. The political parties were split in their opinions. There were also splits within Madison's own party. All of Madison's strength was needed. Dolly's strength was needed, too, but it was of a different kind. She was almost a genius at smoothing out feelings and bringing people into accord with one another.

James urged her to go on with all her social "civilities," for he felt that they were politically important to him and to the nation. Three years later, she could write a letter to her sister, Anna, which proved how right Madison had been about the "civilities." "The Federalists," she wrote, "were all affronted with Madison—refused to dine with him, or even come to the house. But they have changed. Last night and the night before, our rooms were crowded with Republicans, and such a rallying of our party has alarmed them into return. They (the Federalists) came in a large body, last night also, and are continuing calling."

From the first moment of the day that Madison was sworn in, in the new House of Representatives building, Dolly took on the

job of First Lady as though she had been
born to fill it. Both James and Dolly that day
emphasized their political opinions by wearing very *American* clothes. Madison had a
rather rough brown suit of merino wool, wool
that had been grown and sheared, carded and
woven in his own country. Dolly, solemn and
reserved, had a dress of smooth, simple gray
cotton. But something of the child who had
loved baubles and had not been allowed to
wear them showed up, too. The dress had an
elegant train and an open, kerchiefless neck
line. The bonnet was magnificently purple and
white, with curling white plumes.

Jefferson had not yet moved out of the
President's House. So the throngs of people
followed the new President from the House of
Representatives to the Madisons' small house
on F Street, jamming into all the rooms to
congratulate and welcome him. Some of them
dubbed Dolly "Lady Presidentess." Some
called her "Queen Dolly." They seemed to
give their approval to her as much as to
James. They had known her now for eight
years and felt almost as though they were ele-
vating their own princess to the rank of queen.

That night the throng followed the Madisons to Long's Hotel, where America's first

Inaugural Ball was held. The crowd was so great that windows had to be broken to let in air. Dolly's costume delighted her admirers, "pale buff-colored velvet, made plain, with a very long train, but not the least trimming, and beautiful pearl necklace, earrings and bracelet." Here she was gay and charming. She held herself regally. Her cheeks were flushed, her eyes vividly blue. Her black hair was bound up beneath a turban of the buff-colored velvet and white satin, with bird of paradise plumes. She stood beside her bowing husband at the far end of the reception hall and, with him, greeted all citizens who came thronging and jostling up to her. The feathers in her turban nodded; the pearls gleamed. Her warm smile included everyone and infected everyone.

A spirit of optimism and gaiety filled the room. The citizens departed with a feeling that, though difficulties might be coming, they could be met jauntily and with fortitude.

That night Dolly did not look like a woman who could be up early in the mornings dressed in a housedress, a kerchief and an enveloping apron, while she attended to her household chores. No one, seeing her in the evenings, would think of her as she usually was during her daytimes. Then she was planning out the work of the servants, supervising it, cutting out clothes to be sewed up, organizing the marketing, seeing that there was wood for the fires, that there were candles for the sconces. Nor would they think of her providing medicines for anyone who might fall sick, readying warming pans to make the beds comfortable, having quills and pens and papers at Jemmy's hand, and keeping herself ready to be his secretary if his usual secretary was away.

She had had many years of learning how to do all these things and how to do them well. But now she had a household task large enough to make all her previous ones look small.

The President's House was hers and Madison's. It was hers not only to live in but to staff, furnish and beautify. Jefferson, of course, took with him the servants and furniture he had brought from Monticello. He left her a nearly empty, enormous stone residence. It was not yet painted white, not yet porticoed. It had no comforts, and few conveniences. Out-of-doors there were the native trees Jefferson had had planted, and the fence Mrs. Adams had complained of was lacking.

Now Congress appropriated money to fur-

nish the President's House. Dolly asked La-
Trobe to advise her on how the money should
be spent and together they went to work on
the drawing room, the Oval Parlor. They put
huge mirrors on the walls so that the crowds
who gathered there would be reflected back
and forth in dazzling repetition. They put yellow satin-damask draperies at the long windows because of Dolly's fondness for yellow
and because she enjoyed rich materials. They
repeated this yellow satin on the delicate
Sheraton sofas and chairs.

They agreed on almost everything, the purchase of table linen, silver and china, the need
for a pianoforte and a guitar. But they argued
about one ornamentation of the dining room.
LaTrobe wanted the portrait of President
Washington to be hung there, and Dolly let
him win his point.

Washington himself had said that the President's House should have the "sumptuousness
of a palace, the convenience of a house, and
the agreeableness of a country seat." Under
Dolly's direction and with Dolly's work, it began to take on these qualities for the first time.
And under Dolly, too, the house began to be
something else for which it was intended and
which, without her, it might never have been.

It became a house that belonged to the people of the United States. They merely loaned it to their President while he was President, and because they had chosen him to be President. The people felt free to visit, comment on and criticize the temporary resident of the house who, although he was the First Citizen, was still just a citizen.

11. QUEEN DOLLY

THE word *embargo* spelled backwards is *O grab me*. Citizens opposed to the Embargo Act had discovered this reverse spelling and had called it the O-grab-me Act. When the later Non-Intercourse Act restricted trade only with Great Britain and France, the people could find no critical nickname for it, but they disliked it almost as much as the complete embargo. The reason for their dislike was obvious. United States trade was mostly with those two excluded countries. So idle ships stood in the harbors with their sails furled and their masts covered with upside-down tar barrels. The dissatisfied citizens called these barrels "Madison's nightcaps."

Then Congress said that if either Great Britain or France would show friendliness to American shipping, the United States would

The Embargo Act kept ships idle in the harbors

be friendly toward that country, but would refuse to be friendly toward the other. The United States would enforce its Non-Intercourse Act severely against the other country. This suited Napoleon. He wanted nothing better than to have the United States arrayed against Great Britain. He tricked President Madison and Congress into believing that he had revoked all his unfavorable decrees. He did not revoke them, and he had not intended to. But the damage was done. The United States showed more open opposition to England. England replied by blockading New York and by impressment of more and more United States seamen. British ships hovered along the Atlantic coast and captured American ships without reason or excuse.

Finally the situation became intolerable. In June of 1812, Madison sent a message to Congress which said that Great Britain had violated American neutral rights and that war should be declared. By this time, Congress no longer represented just the original Eastern states. It also represented the land-hungry people in some of the new Western and Southern states, who eyed Canada and Florida, hoping to gain territory by war. In these new states there were other people who believed that the British were forever stirring up the Indian tribes to battle the Americans and who felt that a successful war would rid them of this problem. All the reasons for thinking that war was necessary or that it would be helpful or profitable were brought to bear. Congress declared war.

James Madison had talked things over with Dolly, and she had sensed what was coming. In March, she had written to her sister Anna, "The war business goes on slowly, but I fear it will be sure." And in the previous November, she had written to a friend in Paris, "We have new members (of Congress) in abundance, with their wives and daughters; and I have never felt the entertainment of company oppressive until now." Yet Dolly could always bounce back. In this same letter she wrote, "I will ask the favor of you to send me by a safe vessel large headdresses, a few flowers, feathers, gloves, and stockings, black and white, with anything else pretty and suitable for an economist, and let me know the amount."

Dolly believed in enjoying life and helping others enjoy it. She also believed that part of her job was to build up public morale by continuing as if war were not coming. So in the pre-war years of Madison's administration, she set up her own pattern of entertainment in the President's House. It was a pattern with the democratic overtones learned from Jeffer-

*Dolly established egg-rolling on the Capitol
lawn*

son and the open-heartedness that was naturally her own.

It was she who began the Easter Monday
parties for the children in Washington. Each
year on that day the children, as guests of Mrs.
Madison, gathered on the Capitol grounds
with their bright baskets of eggs. Urged on by

her, they rolled the painted eggs downhill, competing to be fastest and still not break a shell.

For the ladies of government officials, she established her "Dove Parties" so that the women would be entertained when the men had to have their Cabinet dinners or other government meetings.

For the general public, she gave her weekly levees or receptions. She sent out no invitations for these. Anyone who read the announcement in the *National Intelligencer* that the drawing rooms would open, and who wished to attend, could attend. Most often the guests were members of Congress, heads of departments, judges of the Supreme Court or foreign ministers with their families. There were also "a great number of most respectable citizens and distinguished strangers." The thronging guests would go up to the end of the drawing room where Dolly stood with James, enjoy his formal little bow and her words of cordial personal greeting. Then the guests would wander further among the large, high-ceilinged, candlelighted chambers of the Mansion. They would admire, with a pride of ownership, the red velvet draperies in one room, the yellow damask ones in another, the

Gilbert Stuart portraits of James and Dolly, the nobly proportioned dining room where LaTrobe had placed the portrait of George Washington. Later in the evening, they would remark on the way Dolly herself went from room to room to see that all of her guests were comfortable and content. They would make mental notes on her shiny black ringlets, her elaborate turbans, her high color. They would listen in on her chatter to report next day to those who had missed the party about her "Irish wit," her "affability," the "ease with which she glided into the stream of conversation and accommodated herself to its endless variety."

They even talked about her visits to Congress when she and the other women would go to listen to the debates there. Once, when Dolly visited Congress, a quite distinguished orator, Mr. Pinckney, was just about to sit down at the end of his speech. When he saw her, he did not sit down, but instead made his speech all over again for her benefit. This time, as a commentator said, he used "fewer arguments," but scattered "more flowers."

Dolly's good food was also a source of comment for her guests, the many different kinds

of cakes, the jellies, the macaroons, the West
Indies fruits being passed about on silver trays,
the punch bowl, the red and white wines, the
tea and coffee. These foods were familiar to
all. But there was one sweet that was new to
most of them. When Dolly served it, they discussed it next day, they recorded it in their
diaries, they wrote letters to distant relatives
about it. It was a delicious cold confection
Dolly served. They called it "ice creams."

As part of all her entertainments, Dolly also
had her parrot. This was a wise, bright-colored,
talkative bird. It was loved by her, by her call-
ers and by all the children who knew her. And
at many of the informal social events she had
her snuff, generously offered from the small
box she carried to the numerous guests who
enjoyed partaking.

In spite of the apparent ease with which
Dolly met so many different people, she must
have done some trembling inside. For she had
a little trick, at small gatherings, to help her
with strangers. One young man noticed that
she always came into her drawing room with
a book in her hand. Observing this once again,
he said, "Still you have time to read."

"Oh, no," she said, "not a word; I have this

book in my hand—a very fine copy of *Don Quixote*—to have something not ungraceful to say, and, if need be, to supply a word of talk."

Yet the trick offended no one, as her other mannerisms offended no one either. This same young man said of her, "My awkwardness and terror suddenly subsided into a romantic admiration for the magnificent woman before me."

The book, as she used it, made some people think that she did not ever really read. However, Parson Weems, well thought of at that time as a writer and historian, begged her to be the patron of a volume he wanted to reprint and asked for "the powerful aid of your recommendation." As he put it, "I had rather have a few lines from Mrs. Madison than from a whole Bench of Bishops." Furthermore, many of her letters to friends and relatives mentioned books she had enjoyed which they might enjoy or asked them to send her new ones which they could commend.

In the November after the declaration of war, the time came to elect a new President. Madison's party nominated him unanimously. The opposition nominated De Witt Clinton. There was a bitter, hard-fought campaign. But when the electors voted, Madison was re-elected by a wide majority. He was President again in spite of what some people called "Mr. Madison's war."

At this time, Jefferson said of him, "I can say conscientiously that I do not know a man in the world of purer integrity, more disinterested and devoted to genuine Republicanism, than himself; nor could I, in the whole scope of America and Europe, point out an abler head."

Madison won the election on his own merits, but his chances were bettered by having a wife who had been described as "uniting to all the elegance and polish of fashion, the unadulterated simplicity, frankness, warmth and friendliness of her native character."

The second inauguration was a quiet one, but a crowded one, too, because "the little man was accompanied on his return to the palace by the multitude; for every creature that could afford twenty-five cents for hack-hire was present." Although the day was sunny, the mood of the people was somber, with the anxiety of not knowing what lay ahead. A parade of soldiers for the occasion was a reminder that times might well be sad and discouraging.

Yet the war, in its beginning, seemed far away. Much of the battling was at sea. Most of the land warfare was in distant Canada. It did not touch people too closely. Soon, however, they began to hear of astounding naval victories. The *Essex* captured one British ship

The American Constitution *defeated the British* Guerrière

after another and regained several American ships. The *Constitution*, "Old Ironsides," won its skillful, daring battle with the *Guerrière*. The bravery, expertness and seamanship of the Americans were being tested and proven. Navy morale was high.

While the Americans rejoiced, the British were dumbfounded. And the London *Times* told just how dumbfounded they were:

> "A third British frigate has struck to an American. . . . This is an occurrence that calls for serious reflection; this, and the facts stated in our paper of yesterday, that Lloyd's list contains notices of upward of five hundred British vessels captured in seven months by Americans: five hundred merchantmen and three frigates! . . . Anyone who had predicted such a result of an American war this time last year would have been treated as a madman or a traitor. He would have been told, if his opponents had condescended to argue with him, that long ere seven months had elapsed the American flag would have been swept from the seas, the contemptible navy of the United States annihilated, and their marine arsenals rendered a heap of ruins. Yet down to this moment not a single American frigate has struck her flag."

One night there was a brilliant ball in

Washington to celebrate the many naval victories. All of Washington society was there. A
military band in bright uniform played for the
dances. The ladies with their gently-moving
fans, their swaying feathers and their sweeping trains were escorted into the ballroom.
Each lady had a gloved hand on the arm of
her escorting "gallant." Each gallant had his
dancing shoes, his silken coat, his wig or powdered hair or queue. There were curtsies and
bows and the pretty steps of the minuet and
the gavotte. There was the "slide-hop" gaiety
of the less formal dances.

But suddenly everything stopped. A young
American naval lieutenant had burst into the
ballroom. He was carrying a flag. He announced that the British thirty-eight-gun frigate, *Macedonian,* had surrendered to Captain
Decatur who now sent dispatches and the
Macedonian flag as a trophy.

People waited and watched to see what the
young lieutenant would do with the flag. No
one was prepared for what he actually did do.
He looked for Dolly. Then, finding her, he
crossed the floor to where she stood and, kneel-
ing, laid the flag at her feet. His whole manner
made it known that he was presenting the
token of success to "Queen Dolly."

The lieutenant laid the flag at Dolly's feet

Dolly blushed, trying to be gracious, actually feeling displeasure. She was perfectly willing to be a most important person in

119

James's life; she was even willing to be a most important person in the life of the Federal City, but she had no wish to be singled out to this degree nor to be treated as the one to whom the trophies belonged. She knew she was not a queen. She knew she was the wife of an elected President.

12. BRITISH INVASION

IF DOLLY MADISON had never done anything else in her life, she would be remembered for what she did on Wednesday, August 24, 1814. She would also be remembered for the cool-headed, steady way in which she did it.

Victories at sea had been plentiful since the start of the War of 1812. American ships had also had some defeats. But the American army, which had become soft and stale in the thirty years after the end of the Revolution, began the new war with more defeats than victories. The quality of the men in the ranks had not changed, but the leadership was poor, with officers elderly and incompetent or unseasoned and blundering. As a result, the British could take the offensive in the land war. Also, they could and did blockade the Eastern seaports. This, combined with the British raids, brought scarcities and commercial hardships. It made the pro-British Federalists more pro-British. It made the anti-war party more eager than ever to tie the hands and slow up the work of the Madisonites who were trying to give the country a stronger army, better preparations, larger money appropriations and a greater realization of dangers.

Long before, while James had been Secretary of State, Dolly had once written to him, "You know I am not much of a politician, but I am extremely anxious to hear (as far as you think proper) what is going forward in the Cabinet." In 1812 and 1813, Dolly was among the few who understood what serious damage the British could do to the United States. She might, as she did, continue her entertaining, but she was aware of what was going on. In the spring of 1813, she spoke of "the fears and alarms that circulate around me," of the fact that the city of Washington was expecting a visit from the enemy, of the "considerable efforts for defense." And she said, "I therefore keep the old Tunisian saber within reach." She knew that British officers in disguise were circulating freely in the city. She knew that there were plans afoot which involved her personally. These plans called for the British to enter the city and to burn the President's residence and offices. She carried this knowledge for over a year without letting it unnerve her. In a larger and more mature way, she was as she had been when her father's business troubles started. She was support to Madison when needed, but she did not try to thrust herself in where she could do nothing.

Finally, in the summer of 1814, British ships carrying an expeditionary force of several thousand troops anchored in Chesapeake Bay. Many of the soldiers in this force were experienced ones who were no longer needed to fight in Europe against France because Napoleon had abdicated. Their leader was the capable General Ross. They were backed up with a fleet of twenty-one British vessels, commanded by Admiral Cockburn. Both the Admiral and the General made open threats that they would invade the city of Washington. Dolly had previously heard, and none too favorably, of this Admiral who had said "that he would make his bow at my drawing room very soon." But she had said, "I do not tremble at this, but feel hurt." And her hurt was not for herself as an individual, but that the dignity and prestige of the United States should be ridiculed and endangered. Nor did she feel hurt in a weak and helpless way. She described herself as "always an advocate of fighting when assailed, though a Quaker."

She was soon to be assailed. For after a short time, the force in Chesapeake Bay was suddenly no longer a force in ships. The troops landed. Four thousand strong, they began to march toward Washington. They were intent upon the orders they had been following all summer "to destroy and lay waste such towns and districts upon the coast as you may find assailable."

News of the approach was brought to the White House. Hasty preparations to defend the ill-prepared city were put under way. A disorderly and badly timed argument began as to who was in charge of preparations. The Secretary of War said it was his job; General Winder said it was his. Madison knew he must settle the argument and superintend the preparations himself. He immediately left to go outside the city where the troops were being placed and the defenses being set up. He took most of his Cabinet with him, and he told Dolly to await his return.

He also told Dolly to be prepared to give the Cabinet members dinner the following day or the day after, to take good care of herself and by all means to safeguard and protect the valuable government papers, which must not be destroyed nor allowed to fall into enemy hands. He said that he would keep in touch with her and let her know exactly what was taking place. He inquired anxiously whether she had the courage and stamina to be left there alone.

No one knew better than Dolly how unprepared the city was for a serious attack. She realized that there would be no military advantage for the British in overrunning Washington. Yet there had been something so vengeful and mean in the laughing threats against the city that she felt they might be carried out. There would be destruction here merely for the sake of destroying. There would also be destruction because the British had said they wanted revenge for similar vandalism on public buildings by the Americans at York, in Canada.

Rumors began flying around Washington— the British were advancing, they were retreating, they were advancing. They were strong, they were weak, they were stronger than anyone had suspected. Thick and fast the rumors came to Dolly. She heard and saw some things she had to believe. The American Commodore,

Barney, had blown up his fleet of gunboats to prevent their being captured by the British. Soldiers had been encamped as a special guard on the green near the President's house. Now they received their orders to go out to meet the invaders. The whole city emptied of men as the citizens went to join their militia outfits.

Dolly found herself surrounded by people in panic, for the women and children were warned to flee. Families packed their possessions into carriages or wagons and started off. They spoke of "bustle and alarm for the worst that might happen." A woman friend of Dolly's wrote her that she was packing to leave even though she did not know where she could go and had no conveyance in which to travel. Other friends and advisers begged Dolly to set out to join the President. But she had no idea where James was, nor even whether he was safe. She had had two penciled scrawls from him, but they could not truly keep her up-to-date. She did not know how he would find her if she left. She certainly did not know how to find him. The only thing she could be sure of was that if the British should come into Washington, they would probably invade her home, would possibly try to capture her. At this moment, Dolly had more reason than most to give way to panic.

She did not give way to it, deciding that she would not be pushed into terror. She waited, and while waiting, she sat down and wrote a long letter to her sister which tells better than anyone can tell for her, how she felt.

Tuesday, August 23, 1814.

Dear Sister,

My husband left me yesterday morning to join General Winder. He inquired anxiously whether I had courage or firmness to remain in the President's house until his return on the morrow, or succeeding day, and on my assurance that I had no fear but for him, and the success of our army, he left, beseeching me to take care of myself, and of the Cabinet papers, public and private. I have since received two dispatches from him, written with a pencil. The last is alarming, because he desires that I should be ready at a moment's warning to enter my carriage and leave the city; that the enemy seemed stronger than had at first been reported, and it might happen that they would reach the city with the intention of destroying it.

I am accordingly ready; I have pressed as many Cabinet papers into trunks as to fill one carriage, our private property must be sacrificed, as it is impossible to procure wagons for its transportation. I am determined not to go until I see Mr. Madison safe, so that he can accompany me, as I hear of much hostility toward him. Disaffection stalks around us. My friends and acquaintances are all gone, even Colonel C. with his hundred, who were stationed as a guard in this enclosure. French John, with his usual activity and resolution, offers to spike the cannon at the gate, and lay a train of powder, which would blow up the British, should they enter the house. To the last proposition I positively object, without being able to make him understand why all advantages in war may not be taken.

The letter stops here and is taken up again the next day. Meanwhile, Dolly was alone in the large, almost deserted, threatened house. The guard was gone; her husband was gone. There were no other relatives or friends about. There were some of the servants, of course, but they were leaning on her. Even French John, John Sioussat, the servant she had had for so long, did not seem to her too dependable.

Dolly must have had moments of great fright. Yet she knew exactly what she had to do and wanted to do: save important state papers, save the long laborious historical notes

James had written for so many years, and wait here for James.

The waiting for James, the anxiety for his safety, probably caused her as much pain as anything else. He was still, after all these years of marriage her "best friend"; he was still "my dearest husband"; still "my beloved." Also she must have realized that his position was even more dangerous because of his office as President of the United States.

The waiting continued throughout a night in the forlorn, huge, empty house. On Wednesday morning, saying nothing about the night, she wrote again on her letter.

> *Wednesday Morning, twelve o'clock*
> Since sunrise I have been turning my spyglass in every direction, and watching with unwearied anxiety, hoping to discover the approach of my dear husband and his friends, but, alas! I can descry only groups of military, wandering in all directions, as if there was a lack of arms, or of spirit to fight for their own fireside.

While she wrote this, a battle was going on near by. She says later, when she continues the letter, "I am still within sound of the cannon." But when the battle first began, she could not know what was taking place except that there was fighting somewhere close and that the situation was grave and that she was in danger. This was the Battle of Bladensburg. Three thousand enemy troops had advanced for many miles without encountering any resistance. However, the Americans were gathering their forces where the British, marching toward Washington, would have to pass. By the time the British arrived at Bladensburg, the Americans had brought together seven thousand troops, militiamen from all over, the sailors from the blown-up gun boats, a few of the regular army. It was a diverse, untrained, poorly equipped army waiting to encounter the seasoned, disciplined troops from Europe. The Americans had the advantage of position, but that was the only advantage they did have. Their general, Winder, was a bungler. Their preparations for defense had been hasty and crude.

Madison and most of the Cabinet witnessed the battle. They saw the Americans routed and saw them retreat in disorder to Georgetown. Only Commodore Barney was left with his sailors to hold back the enemy in land fighting. The British routed the sailors, too, and set up camp less than half a mile from the national capital.

Panic took over in the city. Although many women and children had left the day before, others left now. More wagons were filled with household goods and sent out. Tired, frightened soldiers, trying to find and rejoin their scattered regiments, wandered through town looking lost and bewildered. Tired, frightened messengers carried messages back and forth but could scarcely answer the constant questions, "What's happening?" "What should we do?" "Where is safety?" Frightened servants hid their heads and moaned. Alarmed householders, who could not find a way to leave, also hid.

Madison did not come back to the city. After the defeat at Bladensburg, he went on with the troops to Georgetown. Here he heard that the British were now threatening to capture him, that they thought it would be a fine joke to imprison the President and his Cabinet. He was afraid that their joke might extend to trying to capture the President's wife as well. He sent word to Dolly that she must abandon their house at once before the roads to Georgetown became choked with retreating Americans, before the other roads became hazardous with advancing British.

But Dolly did not leave right away. She was fearful but still able to function calmly. By three o'clock in the afternoon she was getting everything ready for departure, but was still determined to wait until Madison returned. At the same time she went on with her letter. Apparently she wrote this section bit by bit as things happened.

> Will you believe it, my sister? we have had a battle or skirmish, near Bladensburg, and here I am still, within the sound of the cannon! Mr. Madison comes not. May God protect us! Two messengers, covered with dust, come to bid me fly; but here I mean to wait for him. . . . At this late hour a wagon has been procured, and I have it filled with plate and the most valuable portable articles belonging to the house. Whether it will reach its destination, the Bank of Maryland, or fall into the hands of the British soldiery, events must determine. Our kind friend, Mr. Carroll, has come to hasten my departure, and in a very bad humor with me, because I insist on waiting until the large picture of General Washington is secured, and it requires to be unscrewed from the wall. This process was found too tedious for these perilous moments; I have ordered the frame to be broken,

Washington's portrait was removed from the wall

and the canvas taken out. It is done! and the precious portrait placed in the hands of two gentlemen of New York for safekeeping. And now, dear sister, I must leave this house, or the retreating army will make me a prisoner in it by filling up the road I am directed to take. When I shall write again to you, or where I shall be tomorrow, I cannot tell!

DOLLY

She did leave then, but she did not want to. She said, "I confess that I was so unfeminine as to be free from fear and willing to remain in the *castle*. If I could have had a cannon in every window, but alas! those who should have placed them there fled before me, and my whole heart mourned for my country." She had left finally only because of a messenger clattering up to the house on horseback and crying, "Clear out, clear out. Armstrong has ordered retreat!"

Armstrong was the American Secretary of War. His word sounded ominous. Dolly called her maid, Sukey, and together they gathered up the last of the things to be taken with them. Then they hurried away to the waiting carriage and coachman. One Washington woman later reported that she saw them flying full speed through Georgetown, accompanied by an officer carrying a drawn sword.

Dolly did not leave any too soon. The British were in the city two hours after she left it.

They declared they "intended to destroy the public buildings and shipping and then march to Baltimore." They came first to the President's House. They walked insolently through and inspected the interior. Afterward they told that they had seen a dining table set for forty people and a dinner (Dolly's dinner for the Cabinet) smoking on the stove. They carried off minor trophies, a cushion belonging to Dolly and a hat belonging to James. But they would not take major ones because these were public and must be destroyed as tokens of victory.

They went away then and began their ruthless destruction. They set fire to the Capitol building, perhaps figuring that this was more "official" than Madison's residence and so should come first. When the blaze was enormous, they returned to set fire to the President's home, too. An eyewitness has described how they did it:

> Fifty men, sailors and marines, were marched by an officer, silently thro' the avenue, each carrying a long pole to which was fixed a ball about the circumference of a large plate,—when arrived at the building, each of them was stationed at a window, with his pole and machine of wild-fire against it, at

the word of command, at the same instant the windows were broken and this wild-fire thrown in, so that an instantaneous conflagration took place and the whole building was wrapt in flames and smoke. The spectators stood in awful silence, the city was light and the heavens reddened with the blaze!

When the fire had done its work to the President's House, "not an inch, but its crack'd and blacken'd walls remained." All the contents of the house, valuable for beauty, valuable historically or valuable sentimentally, had been lost forever. Nothing had been saved except the precious and secret papers, the silver,

The British set fire to the President's home

some few small "portable" treasures, and the Stuart portrait of Washington. And these had been saved only because of Dolly.

She had had time to make a choice of what would be stowed in the wagons and what must be sacrificed to the enemy. Her velvet and satin dresses, her French turbans, her embroidered slippers, all the well-loved frivolities, were left behind. One loved foolishness she did take care of. The parrot was sent for safekeeping to a friend who was not in public life and who, therefore, had a house which would probably not be molested.

13. THE WANDERERS

THE parrot was safe and well when Dolly returned to Washington three days later. In the meantime, the wife of the President of the United States experienced unbelievable frights and hardships and adventures. Some of the details of the adventures are difficult to learn because Dolly refused to see herself as a heroine. In the only comment she ever wrote on it, she merely said, "I remained nearly three days out of town." She was vehement about the enemy, saying of the American soldiers, that she "wished we had ten thousand such to sink our enemy to the bottomless pit." But she had little to say about herself.

For a while Dolly did not know that James had come to rescue her only a few moments after she herself left the city. He had galloped up to their house, found that she was gone, and galloped away again. But they did not meet on any of the roads that were crowded with other hurrying, frightened refugees. Nor did Dolly find anyone who could tell her for sure where her husband was.

She learned later that he had spent the night at a house on the Potomac River with the men who were guarding him against capture by the British. She herself, with her carriage driver, her military guard of one and her maid, came to a military encampment where some soldiers gave her their tent for the night.

The next morning, she drove on toward Georgetown and crossed the river by ferry. She was beginning to be tired so she stopped for a brief rest at the home of a Mrs. Love whose husband was in the army. The hospitality here deceived her into believing she would find it everywhere. But a few hours later, she discovered how terribly wrong she was.

This discovery came at a public inn. Exhausted, she and Sukey walked in and started upstairs. Someone told the innkeeper's wife who it was. The woman went to the bottom of the stairs and screamed hysterically, "Miss Madison! You come down and go out! Your husband has got mine out fighting, and you shan't stay in my house; so get out!" Dolly could not believe that people still blamed Madison for the war, but she could understand why they would turn against him when things were going so tragically. She could also understand that this woman's anger and fear could make her as dangerous as the British. So, tired as she was, Dolly hurried back to the carriage again and on with her journey.

Finally, she arrived at the place where she and Jemmy had arranged to meet if they could. This was a place deep in the Virginia countryside, the home of a friend, Mrs. Minor. After a short wait, Madison also arrived. That was refreshment enough for Dolly. She had found him safe at last, and they could exchange stories of all that had befallen each of them since their separation. But even James did not know the details of what had gone on in Washington after the British entered it.

The Madisons had heard of the flames climbing toward the sky the previous night. They knew it was the public buildings that had been set afire. They did not know, and there was no one there to tell them, of the rescuing hurricane.

The hurricane had struck Washington at just about the time that Dolly was being ordered out by the angry wife of the innkeeper. It had come up rather suddenly and was extremely violent. Throughout the city, trees were ripped up, roofs ripped off, fences torn to pieces. One excited Washingtonian said, "It fairly lifted me out of the saddle, and the horse which I had been riding I never saw again." One British soldier claimed, "two pieces of cannon . . . were fairly lifted from the ground and borne several yards to the rear." The high wind was followed by torrents of rain. The rain and wind did what the disorganized American Army had been unable to do to the British. The enemy was discouraged, frightened and defeated by the storm. On Thursday night, the invaders broke up camp and returned to their ships.

But Dolly and James knew nothing of this. In the middle of the night, a messenger arrived at Mrs. Minor's house with the false news that the British were assembling for attack very near that house. All felt that the President must go elsewhere for safety. By then it was raining. Nevertheless, President Madison and his protectors went out to hide for the rest of the night in the woods.

The next day he dismissed his incompetent Secretary of War, Armstrong, and appointed

Monroe in his place. Then he hastened off himself to supervise the reorganization of the scattered troops. He wrote a note to Dolly to tell her the news and what she should do. But Dolly, now that she had been forced to part from James again, had pushed on alone. She had, furthermore, disappeared into the woods, and the messenger could not find her.

One reason she could not be found was that she had disguised herself. Her various alarms of the past two days had made her believe she had better not be recognizable as Mrs. Madison. Certainly this was true unless she wanted to risk capture by the British and insults from some Americans who might turn her over to the British. The disguise she chose was that of a poor farm woman. To make the disguise real, she had to give up Sukey and the carriage. She traveled in a farm wagon with two armed guards dressed as humbly as she was. In a way, she probably had fun out of being in disguise. But, typically, she did not think of this as anything very important to other people, for she never wrote any letters or told any stories about it. Only one of her farm-woman adventures is known. The wagon came to a ferryboat which crossed the river. Dolly and her companions asked for passage. But the

ferryman had been detailed to accept only
military men or government officials, or people
who could be of some use to the war cause.
He said, "No." Dolly was forced to tell him
who she was. The dumbfounded man would
not believe her at first, for her disguise was so
good. But he finally let the wagon and its
passengers go across.

The weary journey came to an end when
Dolly learned that the British had evacuated
the city and that it was safe for her to return.
She came back with no fanfare and drove to
the home of her sister, Anna Cutts. She was
there waiting for James when he, too, came
back.

The Federal City to which they had returned was heartbreaking. Only a few private
houses had been touched. But almost all public buildings were in ruins—the Capitol, the
President's House, the Treasury buildings, the
Arsenal. What little had been saved of them
had been saved by the hurricane which had
put out the fires and had frightened away the
British. But the hurricane had also added to
the general look of desolation by tearing down
trees and fences, ripping away roofs, and kill-
ing cattle and horses.

The burning of the Capitol meant that every

book in the first Congressional Library was destroyed. Only through Dolly had the nation been able to preserve its most important documents and papers.

At first, there was great discouragement about the rebuilding of the burned and flattened city. Philadelphia offered to become the capital again, and many citizens felt that this was advisable. But James Madison set to work at once to recreate Washington. His calm, his energy and his belief in rebuilding soon had others following him.

However, the President of the United States and his wife were homeless. It would be a long time before the empty shell that had been the Executive Mansion could be made livable again. And by that time, James's term in office would be over. The rebuilt house would look very different, for it would be painted white— the only way to cover the black, disfiguring marks of fire on the stone walls. The white paint would give it a new name, a permanent name, the White House.

But because the Executive Mansion houses the President, the place that Dolly and James took over became this Mansion for a while. They moved into a fascinating Washington residence, called Octagon House. The affairs of government were carried on from there. And Dolly, once again, was in a position where she had to start a new life.

A new song must have been of help to her in starting it. The British moved on toward Baltimore. They bombarded Fort McHenry. But this time, American preparations were better. American fortification withstood the bombardment, and the next morning "our flag was still there." Francis Scott Key, who had watched the British attack, wrote what he saw and what he felt about American survival in "The Star Spangled Banner."

14. END OF THE WAR

A GREAT American military leader was becoming a hero during the War of 1812. This was Andrew Jackson, who was called "Old Hickory" by the admirers of his toughness and "Sharp Knife" or "Pointed Arrow" by the Indians whose uprisings he put down.

He had been a fighter since he joined the revolutionary army at thirteen. He had started as an unschooled boy from the backwoods. Then he had become a practicing lawyer, a Congressman and a Senator from Tennessee, a Tennessee Supreme Court judge, and a major general in the Tennessee militia. In 1812, he had assembled twenty-five hundred volunteers and had offered them with his services to the federal army. His offer was accepted. Later the Secretary of War ordered him to disband this force, but he had refused and had marched his troops back home. Eventually he had been commissioned a major general in America's regular army.

In everything he was an extremist. He was willful, powerful, easily-angered, violent, crude. He was as totally honest as he was fearless. For his one-track mind, there were no in-betweens. He hated or loved everyone he knew, and everyone he knew hated or loved him.

Jackson was also an individualist. During the days of powdered wigs, he had gone about Washington with his rough queue tied by a snake skin. During his days as judge, he had leaped down from the bench, caught a desperado with his bare hands and arrested him. While fighting one of his many duels, he was badly wounded. But he stood upright beside his wounded opponent until the man was carried away so no one could say he had lost the fight. His spelling and grammar were so original that critics said his letters "would make the better-educated angels weep."

Jackson was first recognized as an exceptional military man in 1814. The Creek Indians had been wasting needed American manpower, but in that year he brought the Creek wars to a spectacular and decisive end.

He became unquestionably one of the greats in January, 1815, when he commanded the sharp-shooting, resourceful, motley troops at New Orleans. Here he won such an overwhelming victory from the British that everyone realized this would be the last major battle of the war.

Victorious in the Battle of New Orleans, the Americans felt that the war had wound up in a blaze of glory. They were sure that the honor of the country, so threatened with the burning of Washington, was restored. The people of the West believed there had never been a general so magnificent as Jackson. People all over the country clamored for recognition for him.

Jackson had been unfriendly to Jefferson because Jefferson opposed Burr. He was likewise not too friendly to Madison. But the Madisons knew the time had come to give the hero his due. The government invited him to Washington. He arrived, and the entire city went wild over him. Dolly gave him a public reception at her house, although the Madisons had had to move again and were living in a fairly small place at the end of those adjoining residences called the Seven Buildings.

The new house had already become well

Children liked to watch Dolly with her parrot

known because of Dolly's habit of feeding the
parrot near the window. The children of the
city would gather outside to watch, fascinated,
and to listen and laugh when Dolly made him

talk. Now with the party for Jackson, the grandest party she ever gave for anyone, that house became even more a spot to gaze at with wonder and delight.

The night of the party, people put on their best clothes to honor Jackson and to be part of the dazzle. They jammed the house to see and be near the hero in his general's uniform with the stiff high-collared coat and the huge gold epaulets. Those who could not crowd into the house stood outside, waiting for a glimpse of him. They peered in, squeezing and jostling, and looking with awe at the glow of the windows where Dolly had stationed liveried servants holding flares or tall lighted tapers in silver candelabras.

Jackson must have felt grateful to Dolly. For when Madison died, many years after this reception, and Jackson was President, he sent Dolly a letter of sympathy that was more than an official message. It expressed his high opinion of a great man and his sympathy for a great woman.

With all the noisy, widespread enthusiasm about the Battle of New Orleans, no one realized immediately that this battle was not what had actually ended the war. A peace treaty, the Treaty of Ghent, had been signed two weeks before the final fighting at New Orleans. But news crept slowly by way of messenger and sailing ships. So, although the treaty was signed in Europe on the day before Christmas, no one in America knew anything of it until the middle of February.

In February, a ship carrying the treaty landed in New York. And special messengers carried the document secretly and swiftly to Washington. A coach and four came thundering down Pennsylvania Avenue. Rumors were already around the city that the treaty was coming so "cheers followed the carriage as it sped on its way to the residence of the President." The coach drew up to the house. Dolly's cousin, Sally Coles, stood inside at the head of the stairs and cried out, "Peace! Peace!" All in the house "went crazy with joy." Soon the place was crowded with visitors. Madison was busy upstairs with the Cabinet, studying the terms of the agreement. He did not have time to share in the celebration. So Dolly ordered wine to be opened and served. She received and returned the hearty handclasps, the congratulations, the relieved smiles. The people who came were of both political factions, but there were no differences now. One of the guests said, "Such a joyful time was never seen in Washington."

After the celebration quieted down, it was many weeks before the people realized how little had been granted the United States in that treaty. Only the heads of the government and those most interested in national affairs understood the peace terms. The war had been going on for nearly three years; the peace negotiations had been underway since August, 1814. Yet the treaty said nothing about any of the neutral rights for which the war had been fought, nor a single word about impressment or blockades, or illegal searching of ships.

Oddly enough, the citizens were not angry with Madison over this treaty as many had been over the war. They knew, with restored national pride, that the American show of ability and victory at the Battle of New Orleans held more insurance for their future than any treaty. They rejoiced over this proof of the worth of their army, and over the sea battles which had proved the worth of their navy. They rejoiced over something else although they were not quite sure what that something else was. It was a feeling of unification, a feeling of all of the United States accomplishing together. The West, added since the Revolution, had shown that it was part of the Union and that it was as strongly national as the East. The East had shown that it could work with the West and the South.

When Madison finished his second term, the results of this unity were being felt. The United States was already on the threshold of "the era of good feeling."

Dolly added her bit to the good feeling in her own particular way. On the last New Year's Day that James was President and she First Lady, she gave one of her memorable receptions. Crowds poured in with their New Year's wishes, hoping perhaps that Dolly would repeat something as eye-catching as an earlier party dress. Then she had worn an ermine-trimmed, rose satin gown with "gold clasps and chains around her waist and arms." On her head there had been a white satin turban trimmed with a gleaming crescent and with tall, curling ostrich feathers.

At the final reception she again wore the towering plumes, but her dress was not described. Perhaps it was one of her famous yellow satin dresses. Perhaps it was the full-trained lemon satin one that was brocaded heavily in silver and draped over a white satin skirt. That one had an underskirt elaborately embroidered in roses and forget-me-nots.

But if Dolly did wear the forget-me-nots that day, they were unneeded. During the past sixteen years her personality had contributed directly to political harmony. For sixteen years she had been radiant, friendly and warm to the people she knew well. She had been a bright star to those who looked at her from a distance. She had given practicality and good humor and deep affection to her husband when he was Secretary of State and later President. Now these years had added up. As the Madisons retired from Washington, Dolly did not need forget-me-nots, embroidered, or symbolic, or real.

15. MONTPELIER, VIRGINIA

ANOTHER of Dolly's new lives began when Madison's term in office ended. Again, there was so much to look back on, so much to look forward to! For now the ex-President and his wife were returning to Montpelier, not for a brief period, but to stay. They were exchanging the excitement and the effort, the gaiety and the tremendous responsibility of the Federal City for the hazy peace of the Blue Ridge Mountains. In Virginia, Dolly would need her simple housedresses more often than her ball gowns. James would spend his time recording history instead of making it. Both would be plantation superintendents. Dolly would reign in the house, in the household work sheds and in the flower and vegetable gardens, James would reign over the cattle and crops. Their world would shrink at the same time that it grew bigger. For now they were no longer the servants of the nation. They were its private citizens, entitled to live as they pleased.

They both were tired when they packed up the accumulated objects of the years and left Washington. But refreshment and vigor were waiting for them in the mountains. Jemmy had been called "a withered little apple-john." He was wiry though, and, even at the age of sixty-six he could spring back from fatigue of both mind and body. He sprang back at Montpelier.

Madison could find peace in retirement because he felt easy about the nation. He had proposed Monroe as his successor, and Monroe had been elected. Madison's own eight years in office had been ones of turbulence. There had been the threat of war, the coming of war, the opposition to war, the ups and downs in national spirit during the war, the victory, the treaty which yielded no point in the prewar arguments. Madison had always been a thinker rather than a doer. He had not been a great wartime leader. In his last two years of stewardship, however, the beginnings of national recovery had taken place. He could predict further recovery under the new administration.

Madison also found peace and vigor in retirement because he had many different tasks waiting for him. One was to go on with improvements at Montpelier. He had begun enlarging and remodeling the house years before. Now he could continue. Both Dr. Thornton and LaTrobe were called in to help him.

Montpelier

Dolly was consulted and listened to. Everyone wanted to keep the clean rectangle of the original house, the wooded knoll on which it stood and the wide sweeping view of the mountains to which it looked. A simple, spacious hallway ran from the front to the back of the house. On either side of the hall were two large rooms. A long pillared porch ran across the front. These features remained as the center of the two-story mansion. One-story wings were added. The house remained beautiful and became large. This largeness was fortunate.

For one thing, Madison's mother was still alive. And James, wise and kind, understood that both his mother and his wife would be happier if the two women could live apart even though together. So the old lady had her private wing and her personal servants. She was mistress of her own domain, well cared for and independent. Dolly, likewise, was mistress of her domain. In these circumstances, Dolly could enjoy doing things for her mother-in-law, and the mother-in-law could enjoy having them done for her. When she was nearly a hundred years old, she said gratefully to Dolly, "You are *my* mother now, and take care of me in my old age."

The largeness of the house was fortunate in another way. The place could accommodate its many visitors.

When the Madisons retired to Montpelier, they were not aware that they would remain in Orange County for the next twenty years. But they must have been able to guess that wherever they went, others would follow and that they could not possibly be tucked away by themselves. The forceful and creative men and women of the day would still flock around them.

Visitors came for many reasons. Relatives and friends came for sociability and renewal of old ties. Men in political life sought advice and mental refreshment. Writers of books and of newspaper or magazine articles came for historical and personal material. Reformers wanted to gain a liberal, up-to-date point of view. Neighbors, even though living miles away, came to talk of horses, of new imports in seeds, of new cuttings for plants, of various problems of landowner and builder. The neighbors came for sociability, too.

Thomas Jefferson, the best neighbor, was still interested in anything and everything. He came for all the reasons that everyone else did. He came, also, to discuss the new University of Virginia which he was fostering and where Madison, who was working with him, would one day take over his responsibilities. Sometimes, with hesitation and a pained bewilderment, Jefferson would mention a little of his financial troubles. The plantation he had had to neglect during political life was not doing well. Crops were poor and prices low. Money he had paid out of his own pocket for national purposes during and after the Revo-

lution was not repaid to him. He was afraid
that he might have to sell Monticello. James
listened in sadness, both for his long-time
friend and for himself. He was aware that his
way of living was like Jefferson's and that his
future financial problems would be much the
same.

At the beginning of the retirement to Montpelier, there were no financial problems. Visitors came to stay for days at a time. They had
ridden or driven over difficult roads to get
there. They had had to contend with broken
carriage springs or with wheels up to the axle
in mud. They had had only slight protection
from weather and wind. They expected to be
put up and to be fed. They did not expect the
exceedingly generous, kindly hospitality they
received.

Some twenty or more house guests at a time
would enjoy the Stuart portraits of Madison's
distinguished friends, the busts and plaster fig-
ures in the drawing room, the beautiful lawn,
the formal gardens, the roses. They would sit
down together to the hearty dinners or take
snacks together at the hearty teas. At breakfast, they would have their hot cakes and meat
pies and hams. Their clothes would be fresh-
ened for them; their way to bed would be

*Lafayette's portrait was painted by
Samuel Morse*

lighted by servants with candles; their beds
would be warmed with warming pans. Yet
they never felt too taken care of. One admiring visitor said of her stay at Montpelier: "No

161

restraint, no ceremony. Hospitality is the pre-
siding genius of this house and Mrs. M. is
kindness personified."

And all the visitors, if they were people
whom Madison liked and respected, would tell
of the wonderful, free-flowing, informative
conversations there. Yet if the visitors were
those who did not particularly interest Madison, they might find him cold, silent and
withdrawn.

One of the Madisons' most enthusiastic visitors and one whose visit they thoroughly enjoyed, was Lafayette. The Battle of Bunker
Hill was fifty years past by that time, and a
monument was to be dedicated at the site of
the battle. Lafayette was invited to come to
America to lay the cornerstone. Before the
dedication, he went to Montpelier to spend
some time with his old friend and fellow-revo-
lutionary, James Madison.

He landed first at New York. There, in the
harbor, Fort Lafayette saluted him. Proces-
sions and parades and cheering citizens turned
out to honor him and to thank him. The United
States Government showed its gratitude by
giving him a gift of Florida land and two hundred thousand dollars.

As part of the celebration, Lafayette's portrait was twice painted by the prominent painter and future inventor, Samuel F. B. Morse. The aging Marquis looked imposing in his long yellow trousers, his high white collar and stock, his coat cut away from a spick white vest. He had grown heavy since his previous trip to America. His dark brown hair was thick. His slightly bulging eyes were still inquisitive, still seeming to look for adventure.

At Montpelier, Lafayette and a large group of people traveling with him were greeted even more warmly than most of the Madisons' visitors. The two old friends, general and statesman, had much to reminisce about. They must also have exchanged excited talk about the unbelievable progress of the United States in the half-century that they had known one another. Aside from everything else, there were now ten million people in the country. There were twenty-four states. The pioneer push to the West had begun and was continuing. A steamboat had gone up the Hudson River, traveling 150 miles in thirty-two hours. After the fire in Washington, Jefferson had sold his library of some nine or ten thousand volumes to Congress to form the nucleus of the Congressional Library. The Erie Canal, often called "Clinton's ditch," was nearly finished. Soon passengers would have comfortable travel from Buffalo to New York in boats drawn by horses walking along a towpath. These boats would take only five days to make the trip and would have wooden shelves to sleep on. The city of Baltimore had all its streets lighted with gas lights. A railroad was being planned which would be drawn by horses along wooden rails. Washington Irving had written *Rip Van Winkle.* James Fenimore Cooper had written several of the *Leather Stocking Tales,* and William Cullen Bryant had written the poem "Thanatopsis." Webster had brought out his *Compendious Dictionary of the English Language.*

Madison told Lafayette what he himself was working on. He was taking his pages and pages of notes, sheaf after sheaf, getting them in order and copying them out. He was making readable all the day-by-day, detailed account of what had taken place in the Constitutional Convention. For the time was nearing when these secret proceedings could be made public. He was also sorting and classifying his correspondence and memorandums. These covered every item of the history in which he had participated since the establishment of the Constitution. He had planned to do this editing and recopying for years. He had never had time for it before. Now he had the time, and he had Dolly as his secretary. She was industrious, he said, and accurate and faithful. It was a tremendous job, but they would finish it. And when they did finish, they would sell these careful records to Congress. They would benefit themselves this way. But to a far greater degree, Madison knew, they would benefit posterity. They would leave a full and truthful record for future Americans of the days—the men, the thoughts, the ideals, the struggles—which marked the beginnings of their country.

Madison confessed, though, that he and Dolly did not spend all their time here in the country at such serious pursuits. He said that sometimes when the weather was bad and they wanted exercise, they would run races with each other along the sixty-foot portico of their beloved Montpelier. This was when Madison was over seventy and Dolly in her middle fifties.

16. A YOUNG LADY OF SEVENTY OR EIGHTY

IN MADISON'S last years, there were many "trying occasions" for Dolly and James. The death of Jefferson was a severe blow to them. So were the circumstances of poverty in which Jefferson was placed toward the end of his life. So was the realization of their own increasing poverty. Actually the Madisons were "land-poor." The expense of constant visitors was very heavy. Then, too, there was the particular and endless expense of Dolly's extravagant, unproductive son, Payne.

Often, when James and Dolly were alone, they would speak of their concern over Payne, who was fulfilling none of their hopes. He had refused an education and he roved continually, unwilling to settle down. He was attractive. He was handsome. He was liked everywhere he went. But he was undisciplined and self-indulgent. He drank too much. He spent more money than he had, piled up gambling debts he was unable to pay and let Madison pay them for him time and time again. He could have been working as Madison's secretary or have found ample work as overseer of the estate at Montpelier. But he did not care for work. Once in earlier years he had been sent to Europe on a commission with Henry Clay. James and Dolly had rejoiced then that a political career was opening up for him. But Payne's chief contribution to the commission had been to dance at a royal ball with the Czar's daughters.

Although Dolly might be saddened by the actions and absences and failures of her child, she could never stop loving him or trying to help him. Even at the end, when she knew for sure that Payne would never be anything but a disappointment, she said, "Forgive my boy for his eccentricities; his heart is all right."

During Madison's last five years, he was almost crippled by rheumatism. It was so hard for him to get about that he spent all of his time in two rooms of the enormous plantation house. Here, blazing log fires and shawls and covers warmed his shriveled body while his mind drove him to labor hour after hour on his papers. Here Dolly was both his nurse and his secretary, confined but loving, tired but going on.

The spirit in which he handled his illness made it easier to go on. He still saw most of the visitors, still talked of the political present and the political past, of his reading, of his belief in the importance of the papers he was working on, of the University of Virginia, of slavery problems, of crops, plows, horses, cattle. He still had his sense of humor and his dry wit. Once when he was quite ill and was lying down while he talked to a friend, the friend begged him not to try to continue the conversation in that position. "Oh," Madison said with a smile, "I always talk most easily when I lie."

By coincidence, Thomas Jefferson and John Adams had died on the Fourth of July in 1826, and James Monroe on the Fourth of July, 1831. The impression made by this coincidence was so strong that when Madison was very ill in 1836, it was hoped that he could live until that Fourth of July. "But," Dolly's great-niece said, "he died June 28th in the full possession of all his faculties; as serene, calm, and philosophical in his last moments, as he had been in all the trying occasions of his life."

The Madison papers were James's last preoccupation and effort. They were also his last gift to Dolly. His will left them to Dolly to guard and to have published. This will was not only a gift, but a loving compliment. It showed what Madison thought of her intelligence, her understanding of the papers and her industry over them. It also showed that through the sale of them, he wanted her to be as comfortable financially as he could possibly make her. Dolly felt that the will *asked* something of her as well. Her Jemmy had left it up to her to see that his fame was preserved and made known to everyone.

She was glad to have work to do after James's death. Montpelier seemed empty in spite of the visitors who kept coming and the slaves who lived there and the relatives who came to console her. After a while even work was not enough, and she no longer wanted to be isolated on a plantation.

Sometimes she had talked of living in New York or in Philadelphia. But there was only one city where she really belonged. She had lost her heart to the city of Washington, just

as Washingtonians had lost their hearts to her
And so, in 1837, within a year after she became a widow, Dolly Madison returned to the
capital, a permanent resident, a fixture, a
landmark.

Her welcome did not take the form of
torchlight parades or rocket explosions or
cannon salutes, but it might just as well have
done so. In the quiet enthusiasm, in the honors given her, in the active social life, the people of the capital showed what it thought of
this plump, majestic, elderly woman. For the
past twenty years she had been gone from
their midst, but had not been gone from their
minds.

The President gave her the franking priv-
ilege, permission to mail letters and packages
without cost. Congress did something for her
it had never done for any other woman. It
allowed her a seat, not in the gallery with
visitors, but on the floor with the legislators.
After a while, the newspapers carried stories
of the kind of light-hearted love affair that
seemed to be going on between Mrs. Madison
and the whole of Congress. The members
treated her with courtliness and gallantry, not
only because she was the widow of a former
President, but also because of her charm and

liveliness and friendly personality. She responded, dignified and calm, but with a twinkle.

The flirtation with Congress did not, however, extend to business matters. She sold the first batch of Madison's papers to Congress shortly after his death. She called this batch the "debates in the Revolutionary Congress and in the Convention." She delivered them in a red morocco trunk, the only thing large enough to hold them, and received thirty thousand dollars for them. She also received permission to have them published and distributed more widely after Congress made the plates from them. But permission and actual doing were two different things. Dolly had had no business experience. She had no one to advise her. These papers had been painstakingly written out in longhand and copied that way three times to insure against loss. They were testimonies to years and years of labor and the most concentrated thought. But they brought in nothing more than the thirty thousand for a long time. The rest of Madison's works were written and copied the same way. They were his histories and his best reflections on many subjects, but they brought in no money at all for twelve years.

Meanwhile, Montpelier was bringing in nothing either. Dolly knew no more about farming than she knew about business. Madison had foreseen very hard times for Virginia landowners. He could not have stopped them. Dolly could not even delay their coming. Payne gave no assistance. He still spent money wildly. He still lost money in any business venture. He borrowed from his mother but did not repay. He even deceived her by saying he was working on the sale of the papers. Actually he was only living in New York at her expense and with the attempted sale as an excuse.

Dolly was forced to sell some of her Virginia land and later sold Montpelier. In 1848 Congress paid twenty-five thousand dollars for the remaining Madison Papers. Most of it was in a trust fund from which Madison's widow should receive an annual income.

No one knew exactly how simply she lived, for she did not talk about it. But in her later years some of her friends sent her fruits from their trees and delicacies from their kitchens to be sure she would have these things. In return she loaned them her books and her servant, Paul.

Fortunately she owned her little house in

Washington. She brought furnishings to it
from Montpelier. Her French chairs and sofas
and tables gave the Washington house the
same lightness and elegance that her country
place had had. But to Dolly a home was never
a place to have just furniture and fine china
and rich fabrics. It was a place to have people.
The furnishings were only the background to
help her guests enjoy themselves.

And so Dolly blossomed out as a hostess
again. On the New Year's Day after her return to the capital, President Van Buren had
his reception at the White House, newly reno-
vated and redecorated and gleaming white.
The crowds flocked in to see him. But afterward, although there had been no plan for it,
the visitors who left the White House paid a
second call. They turned away from the Mansion and went to the small home in Lafayette
Square to pay their respects to Dolly. From
then on, for the twelve remaining years of her
life, it became traditional on New Year's Day
and the Fourth of July, for Washington society
to call first on the Chief Executive and then
on Mrs. Madison.

At other times Dolly was not alone in the
house. Anna Payne, a niece, lived with her.
Together they were invited to dine with the

various Presidents, with the changing Secretaries of State and other government officials Together and separately, they made their many formal calls, their many informal visits. And soon people said, "It became an honor not only to be her guest, but to be a guest where she was present." Dolly did not go shopping now, but she renewed old friendships and she added as friends, women and men much younger than herself. Dolly liked the young. She felt no differences in age. And young people, when with her, felt no differences either.

The elderly, active, pliant Mrs. Madison also took part in the Washington life that was not social. She kept in close touch with the Sisters of Visitation Academy and was invited to come to the school on the big day each year when "Premiums" were awarded to the prize students. She helped other prominent women raise money to build the Washington Monument and helped collect clothing for the needy.

Then Samuel F. B. Morse invented a way to transmit signals by electricity and also a code for these signals. Morse had not started out as a scientist. He had been a noted painter and one of the founders of the National Academy of Design. After Daguerre, in France, invented a process of photography, Morse had introduced the process into the United States. When he began to talk of "telegraph," of sending messages along wires, some people thought he had lost his sanity. But Dolly could believe in miracles. She was pleased when Congress appropriated money to build an experimental line and especially pleased when Morse invited her to be among the listeners to the first telegram coming through from Baltimore to the Capitol building in Washington. After that first message had click-clicked its message *What hath God wrought!* Morse turned to Dolly and asked her to compose the first return telegram.

It was as natural for Morse to pick her out as first-lady-in-her-own-right as it was for President Polk to do the same on another occasion. Polk selected her from all the guests at one of his large receptions, offered her his arm and took her about the crowded White House rooms so everyone could pay honor to her.

On next to the last Fourth of July of her life, when she was eighty years old, she attended the laying of the cornerstone of the

Washington Monument. Perhaps, as the ceremonies went on, she looked back, seeing the whole span of history which George Washington and his contemporaries had made, seeing James's momentous share in it and realizing how much she herself had participated in the growth of the new republic, but she gave no sign of where her memories were. Perhaps she thought, "This country has come a long way," and then thought, "Yes, and it still has a long way to go." She gave no sign of that either. She stood there in quiet dignity, not pressing herself forward, not making herself too noticeable. She was again, as so often before, part of the background of great and memorable events.

Yet she was noticed. And she was remembered, then and afterward, as far more than background, as a completely feminine person who had been strong, decisive and useful. She was remembered for wit, courage, warmth, responsibility, joyousness, effort, accomplishment.

An old, no longer stylish, no longer gay, no longer necessary woman stood there and was remembered with affection, loyalty and respect.

WHEN IT HAPPENED

1768 Dolly born

1783 Dolly moved to Philadelphia
End of Revolutionary War

1787 Constitutional Convention
Federalist papers (also 1788)

1788 Ratification of the Constitution

1789 First Presidential Election
Bankruptcy of Dolly's father
James Madison in Congress (1789–1797)
The Bill of Rights written by Madison

1790 Philadelphia named temporary capital
Dolly married to John Todd

1792 Washington unanimously re-elected
Laying of cornerstone of White House
Payne Todd born

1793 Yellow fever epidemic
Dolly's second son born
John Todd died

1794 Dolly married to James Madison
Jay Treaty signed

1797 John Adams inaugurated President
Madisons returned to Montpelier for four years

1800 Capital moved to Washington, D. C.
Napoleon gained Louisiana from Spain

1801 Thomas Jefferson inaugurated President
Madison Secretary of State

1803 Louisiana Purchase

1804 Lewis and Clark expedition
Duel between Burr and Hamilton
Dolly's sister, Anna, married
Gilbert Stuart portraits of Dolly and James
Jefferson re-elected

1807 Dolly's mother died

1809 Madison inaugurated President

1812 Madison re-elected
Madison's war proclamation issued

1814 British in Washington

1815 Battle of New Orleans
Napoleon exiled to St. Helena

1817 Monroe inaugurated President
Dolly returned to Montpelier for twenty years

1824 John Quincy Adams elected President
Lafayette visited Montpelier

1825 50th anniversary Battle of Bunker Hill

1828 Andrew Jackson elected President

1836 James Madison died
Van Buren elected President

1837 Dolly returned to Washington
Victoria became Queen of England
Some of Madison's papers were sold to Congress

1841   William Henry Harrison inaugurated President
        Vice-President John Tyler succeeded to Presidency

1844   First telegraph

1845   James K. Polk inaugurated President

1848   The rest of Madison's papers sold to Congress
        Laying of cornerstone of Washington Monument

1849   Zachary Taylor inaugurated President
        Dolly Madison died

Index

LANDMARK BOOKS

WORLD LANDMARK BOOKS